A Bear in My Bed & A Jackal in My Oven

Adventures of an Israeli Wildlife Zoologist

By Avinoam Lourie & Cissy Shapiro

Copyright © 2010

Creative Brilliance / Avinoam Lourie & Naomi K. (Cissy) Shapiro

Illustrations by Yael Kimhi Orrelle

Cover photo by Naomi K. Shapiro

ISBN: 9780945139010

Creative Brilliance
Att: Naomi K. (Cissy) Shapiro
Box 44237
Madison, WI USA 53744-4237
Phone: 608-827-6483
e-mail: cre8vNaomi@gmail.com
www.NaomiShapiro.com

Library of Congress Preassigned Control Number
Lourie, Avinoam & Shapiro, Cissy.
A Bear in My Bed & A Jackal in My Oven
by Avinoam Lourie & Cissy Shapiro
ISBN: 9780945139010 LCCN: 2010925630

Preface

I have known Avinoam Lourie since we received our M.Sc. degrees in Zoology at the Hebrew University in 1972.

While I continued my graduate studies, Avinoam was already busy working as an ichthyologist for the Sea Fisheries Research Station in Haifa, and then directing the zoo in Haifa.

In 1979, he joined Israel's Nature Reserves Authority, heading the Wildlife Conservation Department where he was responsible for all aspects of animal handling, animal damage control; and resolving conflicts between the agricultural sector and hunters.

That also included responsibility for implementing programs envisioned by Nature Reserves Authority founder, Avraham Yoffe, and former assistant Division Head, Uri Tzon, regarding reintroduction of animals formerly found in Israel.

Avinoam was also involved in many of the educational programs for nature conservation throughout the country, and initiated the breeding center and the reversed daylight exhibition at Yotvata Hai-Bar in southern Israel.

He reintroduced onagers in the Negev, and later participated in the reintroduction of the Persian fallow deer and the roe deer when he became director of Carmel Hai-Bar, as well as being involved with many other reintroduction procedures.

In his job helping develop animal damage control methods, Avinoam wrote the first manual on this subject for field workers, as well as coordinating hunting, and regulating the use of natural assets by researchers and educators.

He developed the concept of educational Children's Zoos to teach the young about our nature and wildlife.

When I became Chief Scientist of the Nature Reserves Authority in 1983, the personal and professional relationship between Avinoam and myself grew strong.

We worked closely on many complicated issues regarding hunting, animal damage control, reducing conflicts with nature, and animal handling—and we had to rescue each other many times from delicate situations in dealing with the public, organizations, authorities, and politicians.

It was made so much easier because of Avinoam's elegant manner, as well as his instincts and "friendly persuasion" in dealing with people, while always remaining dedicated to nature conservation and education.

He was so much fun to work with, with his easy-going manner, and taking everything on the light side with a lot of humor, while getting the job done.

Avinoam's work is an important milestone for nature conservation in Israel—and, despite his retirement in 2004, our close friendship continues.

Dr. Eliezer Frankenberg
Former Chief Scientist of Israel's Nature Reserves Authority
Jerusalem, Israel
May, 2010

Foreword

Located at the crossroads of three continents, Israel has no oil... or diamonds... or gold... but our unique population of wild animals is one of the greatest riches anyone could have.

Our small, interesting country is represented by animals from Europe, Asia, and Africa, plus a hitchhiker from America (the blue crab).

At snow-capped Mount Hermon in Israel's north, you'll find European animals such as the Lebanon viper, Hermon viper, snow vole, and the rare Persian squirrel.

Little more than a half hour south in the Jordan Valley, you'll be "in Africa," where you'll find gazelles, hyrax, black francolin, and black cobra. Continue south from there another hour or two and you'll come to the Negev where you'll find desert animals such as the Dorcas gazelle, sand fox, desert hedgehog, Houbara bustard, and the ornate mastigure (lizard).

Over the centuries, some animals of the Holy Land—Syrian ostrich, Syrian onager, and Israel's painted frog—disappeared from the world forever. Others, like the cheetah, sand cat, lappet-faced vulture, and brown fish owl disappeared only from Israel. Others yet, like the sand fox, Syrian speckled frog, Egyptian vulture, and leopard are on the edge of extinction in Israel at this very moment.

On the other hand, rare, thought-to-be-extinct Persian fallow deer (also known as Mesopotamian fallow deer) flourish in Israel again, following an amazing escapade of international intrigue to get them from Iran. Their story continued with a highly successful breeding program in Israel, bringing them from the original four to the largest population in the world today!

We also successfully reintroduced onagers and Arabian oryxes that are now roaming free and flourishing in the Negev.

For such a small country with a high rate of development (and too many wars), it hasn't been easy to keep the animals in balance. Wild boars, ravens, and jackals are now too numerous in Israel and cause a lot of agricultural damage.

New "invaders" such as the common mynah, Indian crow, and ring-necked parakeet, all of which escaped from zoological gardens or were smuggled into the country, continue to damage our fragile ecological system.

While most people are quick to adore and support pandas and dolphins in the world in general, I want them also to learn to love the not-so-beautiful and not-so-cuddly animals—toads, lizards, hyenas, vultures, snakes, and spiders—creatures which are infinitely interesting, play critical roles in the ecosystem, and also need attention.

I hope and believe that a positive attitude and sympathy toward all animals will increase people's love and understanding of each other—wherever they are, and whether they are different in appearance, color, religion, geography, politics, behavior, personality, or philosophy of life.

Avinoam Lourie
May, 2010

About the author

An only child, Avinoam Lourie discovered early that the animals and insects near his house in Jerusalem's Beit HaKerem neighborhood were his friends. The boy spent every moment in the fields, turning over rocks, picking up snakes and scorpions, finding and caring for small animals, and even getting stung into unconsciousness by a swarm of large Oriental wasps.

As he became adept at predicting which creatures would be found under specific rocks, his first job, at age 12, was to provide poisonous snakes and scorpions to researchers at the Hebrew University, which he'd deliver in an unorthodox way— steering his bike with one hand while holding a poisonous snake or box of scorpions in the other!

That love of all living things translated into a B.Sc. and M.Sc. (with distinction) from Jerusalem's Hebrew University, followed by research on new fish that emigrated from the Red Sea to the Mediterranean via the Suez Canal. Later he was made director of the Haifa Zoo, worked for the Israel Nature Reserves Authority at the Yotvata Hai-Bar in the south and Carmel Hai-Bar near Haifa. His job was to save and bring back near-extinct and endangered animals that once thrived in the Holy Land— and release their offspring back into their natural habitats.

Avinoam retired in 2004, and now devotes much of his time telling stories to at-risk children, and relating to children in general by establishing and helping maintain, with the help of the Carmel Rotary Club, "animal schoolyards" for children to learn more about nature and animals in safe, unthreatening environments. He also serves as a volunteer in released-criminal rehabilitation programs.

CONTENTS

Animals Are Our Friends.
Sometimes.

Monsieur Viktor Misbehaves

It was nearly noon when I heard a light knock on my office door at the Haifa Zoo.

In the doorway stood a very thin man with a huge mustache, a wild beard, and a French accent, which I recognized when he said, "Mon nom is Julienne, and I am ze director of ze French Circus zat is now appearing in downtown Haifa."

"You know," he continued, "you have a nice zoo, a small, enchanting zoo, but I notice zat you have no chimpanzees. By chance I have an extra one zat might be a nice addition for you, as it is a quiet female. And you know that a chimpanzee costs several sousand dollars," he added.

For quite a while I had wanted to get some chimpanzees to round out our zoo offerings, so my mind was racing about how to do this.

"It will take me a few weeks to raise money for such an acquisition and to build a proper accommodation for a monkey," I said, "and another thing I have to think of would be a mate for her because monkeys don't fare well socially if they are isolated."

"Non, non, non," the Frenchman interrupted, "I am going to GIVE you a chimpanzee as a present."

A light bulb went on in my head, and I said: "I just thought of a very good temporary solution; I will call the zoo director in Tel Aviv and see if he can keep the new monkey until I set up a proper enclosure for it here."

I called my good friend and counterpart in Tel Aviv right then, and he gave me an immediate, positive response about getting a chimpanzee. "Take it," he whispered. "It's worth more than you think," and if you can't keep it, I will. We need to add a female to our collection, too," he added.

So I turned to the Frenchman and said, "OK, we'll be happy to get this chimp—and we can give you a nice Israeli animal—a gazelle or a young bear—as a present for one of your zoos."

"Non, non," he replied. "I zust want you to do for me a very zimple thing."

"You zee," he went on, "we have to leave ze country and return to France in three days; and we have to leave, for ze time being, our best star, Monsieur Viktor, as he bit a young child who threw a stone at him at the circus. And now, your 'square' veterinarians won't release him until he passes quarantine."

"Please go to ze quarantine center in seven days," the Frenchman continued, "put him in a small box, take him to ze airport, send him to ze address I will give you, and call me when you send him."

My mind was racing. "I didn't even know how to immobilize a chimpanzee if necessary," I was thinking to myself.

The man must have read my thoughts, for he said: "Don't be afraid. Monsieur Viktor is zust a small chimpanzee; just call him and he will come to you and he will be obedient."

(At this stage of my life, I was still very naive, and at that moment, the man opened his shabby coat, took out a brown bottle, and said, "Let's drink to zis agreement.")

As I didn't want the people at the zoo to see us, we both drank from the same bottle, no glasses. And, although it tasted like pure poison to me, he said it was, "one of the best cognacs." And then he left.

Seven days passed.

On Thursday I drove to the quarantine center, and one of the zookeepers went with me. I knocked on the door of the center and told them I came to take the monkey.

The guy there was incredulous. "The monkey?!?" he said. "The devil, I would say."

"Why do you say this?" I asked.

"He made a lot of trouble for us," was the reply.

"He stole the water hose from the cleaner and wet us all; then he threw excrement on us; and many other things. We're

14

very happy to get rid of him, but we're not going to go and get him for you, oh no! We will give you the key and you will take him. He is your baby now."

They gave me the key.

When I approached the cell where they had put the monkey, I saw that "the small chimpanzee" wasn't small at all. As a matter of fact he was quite large—about 170 pounds—and he didn't react to me at all.

All this time, all the quarantine workers were watching, from behind windows with bars! I suspect they were waiting for him to do something bad to me, too.

I looked at the monkey. The monkey looked at me, with a blank expression. His eyes glittered like green lights, and he had a very strange smile.

I was trembling with fear because he was much bigger than I had imagined. The Frenchman had told me, "it is a small, very modest, very quiet chimpanzee," but after I saw his real size and heard what he had done to all these people, I was afraid to show my own fear now.

They obviously had good reason for hiding behind bars, but I couldn't let them know that I was afraid also.

So I called to the monkey.

He didn't react.

I lowered my body, going down on my knees in a submissive gesture. Without looking at his eyes, I called to him in a very soft voice... "Monsieur Viktor, I am your friend," and then I said, "*vien ici*" (come here) in French.

He was so fast, I couldn't even count to two, and he was already hugging me tightly and I felt his moist lips on my cheek.

All the heroes outside applauded.

I put a collar with a short leash around his neck.

With the monkey still embracing me, I carried him out to my small car where my helper was waiting. I put Mr. Viktor gently on the rear seat and I got into the driver's seat.

And then the trouble began!

He must have been spooked by the noise of the engine when I turned it on, because he immediately released a very large pile of soft, smelly excrement on the back seat.

It had such a very strong, sickening odor, we thought we were going to pass out.

Because it was a hot summer day in Haifa, the keeper wanted to open the window to get some fresh air. But I told him to leave it closed because the monkey might run away.

And then the monkey started to play with what he had done on the back seat, and began to smear it all over the car and on our backs.

To make matters worse, we had to stop and wait for a train to pass at a crossing.

Then the keeper said in a low voice, "look what he's doing to me now"—and I saw Monsieur Viktor playing with the keeper's throat from behind, pressing a little—and I saw that the keeper had a hammer in his hand, and he said through clenched teeth, "I'm going to hit him before he strangles me!"

I offered the monkey a carrot that I had brought in my pocket, and he calmed down.

After what seemed to be a particularly long drive, we finally arrived at the zoo.

Monsieur Viktor took my hand and we walked together (like good friends from the movie "Casablanca") to the small cage in which he would wait until his flight two days later.

We had prepared some fruit in the cage to give him a reason to enter.

I told him very politely, "Monsieur Viktor, *allez*, go into the cage."

He didn't react.

I thought maybe he would like to be in the cage together, so I entered first and invited him (very politely) to join me, holding a banana in my hand.

He didn't react.

Maybe the cage was too small.

Maybe he just didn't like the atmosphere.

16

But he didn't come in.

At that point, I made the mistake of trying to pull him inside by jerking on the leash—and, very fast, in a fraction of a second, he pulled his way up the leash and bit my hand.

Because the bite was so painful, I opened my hand and let go of the leash. And Monsieur Viktor ran away, to go "wandering" in the zoo.

(I was mortified to imagine the headlines in the paper the next morning: Big chimpanzee runs away from the Haifa Zoo; walks freely in the nearby Carmel Center; people crying from fear; chimpanzee gets agitated and does damage at a fruit or vegetable market; chimpanzee bites. And the comments that would follow about the stupid zoo director who was running after him, couldn't stop him, and who would be fired the next day—the shame that would come upon the man who was not able to keep his animals under control!!)

In order to avoid hysteria in the zoo, I told the other keepers to send all the people out of the zoo. "Give them a ticket to come back another time," I said, "and be very quiet, so you won't make the monkey nervous."

My hand was still bleeding, but the excitement of the moment probably covered the pain.

I told the zookeepers to stay put, and I edged closer to Viktor, who was now near the wolf cage.

I offered him a plum. As the day was quite hot and he was probably quite thirsty, he came to me, took the plum, and gave me his hand, like we were friends again, and we began to stroll through the zoo together.

My mind was racing about how to resolve the situation, and then I calmly guided us to the zoo's public toilet, because I figured it didn't look like a cage.

As soon as Monsieur Viktor and I entered the toilet together, I kicked the door shut and yelled to the keeper to bring me a syringe with immobilizing medication.

Then we immobilized the big chimpanzee and put him in his cage.

17

That was when I finally realized that my hand was still bleeding, and how dirty and smelly I was from all my activities of the day with Monsieur Viktor.

I changed my clothes, took care of my wound, and relaxed with a large bottle of soda.

That Sunday, we again immobilized Monsieur Viktor, put him into the traveling crate, and I drove to the airport, feeling happy thoughts about finishing my responsibilities with him.

But Monsieur Viktor wasn't done with me yet. The cage was tied to the roof of my car and just as we approached the airport, I thought it started to rain, because I couldn't see anything through the windshield. But it was summertime in Haifa and we don't have any rain in Haifa in the summer. I didn't immediately realize what was happening, but then it dawned on me: It was chimpanzee urine streaming down the windshield from the crate on the roof.

When we got to the airport, I gave the crate to the people there, who insisted on checking the straw in case there might be illicit drugs hidden in it.

It took me more than half an hour to convince them, that if we opened the cage, he might get out into the terminal, we wouldn't be able to catch him again—and they would surely lose their jobs as a result!

I was running all over to get papers and confirmation stamps from all sorts of big shots (and small shots). And I was quite worried that the plane would leave before I was finished.

I finally succeeded in convincing the terminal director that the risk of trouble with Monsieur Viktor was greater than the chance of finding drugs, so he let the monkey fly without checking the straw. We got Monsieur Viktor's crate onto the plane with just a few minutes to spare.

Final thoughts about this experience: If someone offers you a free chimpanzee, they might be making a monkey out of you!

PS You might be wondering what happened to the female monkey that the Frenchman said he would send as a gift for our help with Monsieur Viktor—and here's what happened to "Madame Genevieve."

Madame Genevieve

As a thank you for our "care" of Monsieur Viktor, the French circus guy sent a female chimpanzee to the Tel Aviv Zoo the very next day after he had been in my office to ask me to do the favor.

The Tel Aviv staff tried for quite a long time to put her with a resident troop of chimpanzees, but because she had been isolated from wild chimpanzees from early childhood, she didn't socialize well, causing continuous problems, so they took her out of the group.

Madame Genevieve was either very aggressive or frightened, didn't make any contacts, and the others didn't want her. She was attacked and wounded twice by the males; they didn't let her eat; and she also got a lot of punches from the dominant females in two different chimpanzee cages.

It didn't even work when they tried to put her with a quiet old male. So in the end she was licking her bruises, alone, in a comparatively small cage.

While she was in "solitary confinement" in Tel Aviv, I was still trying to build a proper cage for her at the Haifa Zoo, per my original intention when the Frenchman first met with me.

We really wanted and needed a nice chimpanzee, and I didn't want to compromise on a cage that might not be wide enough or good enough for such a monkey, because they need space, toys, proper vegetation, and so on.

However, before I was finished preparing for her, Madame Genevieve succeeded one day, nobody knew how, to push the zookeeper and run out of the cage, climb quite easily over the zoo wall, run across the road, and enter the apartment of an old Hungarian woman, through the third floor window. It was early morning, and the chimpanzee found and ate a lot of fruits and some cake from the table, and the woman began to scream and cry for help in Hungarian.

Unfortunately for Madame Genevieve and us, the police inspector arrived before the zoo people could get there and use a proper net to catch her. And, because the monkey nearly pushed the police inspector off the balcony, he had to use his revolver on her. And that was her (and our) sad ending.

As we have learned from many sad examples, not all animal stories end happily.

A Scorpion Teaches Me a Lesson

When I was still a student at the Hebrew University (and a self-professed scorpion expert), I was helping one of the professors show the students scorpions in nature.

We chose a very nice area near the Dead Sea for an outing and demonstration about scorpions.

We went at night in order to demonstrate that scorpions glow fluorescently when you shine a beam of UV rays on them; and also to show the students that scorpions were much more abundant than they imagined.

So there we sat, on a small hill in complete darkness. When we turned on our UV torches, the students could see many, many scorpions all around us, glowing with their typical yellow-green fluorescence.

I told the students a bit about scorpion biology, including the scorpions' mating techniques, which go somewhat as follows:

The male holds the female close and dances with her, to and fro, and to the sides, and then kisses her. Their mouths meet, and although they stop holding hands, they really kiss.

Then the male scorpion pastes a small sperm parcel to the ground and pulls the female very carefully over it and has her sit on it, and the sperm goes into a special opening on her body.

Then the male quickly goes away. (If you're a male, this is important, because he is actually smaller and weaker than she is, and he might become a source of food for her if he hasn't danced nicely enough for her satisfaction).

Before scorpion mating was described in zoology books, Walt Disney unknowingly caught this mating dance in his famous film, "The Living Desert," which showed a segment of a

"Charleston" (dance) by a pair of scorpions. That really was their mating dance!

Anyway, that night at the demonstration, I wanted to show the students that scorpions were not aggressive if they didn't need to be—at least that's what I thought then.

So I took one of the scorpions, put it on my lower arm, believing—as my zoology professor had told me—that if you didn't press them or tease them, they wouldn't do anything to you.

The scorpion began to walk up my arm... and then, without any provocation, stung me near the inside of my elbow!

I managed to stammer and utter the following words, "Apparently the scorpions didn't read the book that my professor wrote!"

I felt absolutely mortified; I think the students probably enjoyed what happened, as they were probably already uncomfortable sitting in the dark where they knew there were a lot of scorpions around, and they were happy to see someone more uncomfortable than they were.

Someone brought me ice to put on the bite, and I experienced very severe pain for a couple of hours.

But, to be completely honest, the physical pain was nothing compared to the EXTREMELY painful embarrassment, shame, and humiliation that I felt!

Fight for My Life with a Jealous Roe Deer

Reproduction of roe deer in captivity is not so common. Even when you give them the proper conditions, food, and shelter, it is still a difficult task.

To encourage mating in our breeding nucleus of roe deer, we put one male and one female in each enclosure. We didn't want the males to kill each other, as two males might fight until one of them is dead or runs away.

In 2001, in one of the enclosures at the Carmel Hai-Bar Nature Reserve (Hai-Bar literally means "wild animal"), I observed two new fawns.

Interestingly, the devoted mother didn't keep them together—apparently to protect them if a predator came. She had put one on one side of the enclosure and the other on the other side of the enclosure—both of them in dense vegetation. In fact, when I searched for the young fawns, it took me some time to find them.

One day, I thought that one of the fawns was not holding its head properly, so, without thinking, I entered the enclosure to check on it.

I forgot that I wasn't "the boss" in this enclosure.

The boss was "Albert from Tuscany"!

Albert was about four years old at the time, and these were his first offspring.

I checked the young fawn and saw that I was mistaken. He was ok, and even produced a small baa-ing sound.

And then—it came!!!

I felt a very strong blow to the back of my left leg.

23

I was thrown a few yards by Albert, close to the gate of the enclosure.

The gate wasn't locked, so Albert hit me again and tried to stab me again, with a series of blows to my lower back, and he pushed me out of the enclosure!

Although I felt a very sharp pain in the back of my left leg and I was bleeding severely, I succeeded in grabbing Albert's two antlers with my hands. With his front legs, Albert tried to "make a hole," scraping, pounding and banging his hoofs on the ground.

I remember that his eyes were very glittering and bright; he uttered short "bow-wow" sounds like a dog, and saliva dripped from his mouth. I was aware of his very fast breathing and I could see his muscles contract when he was trying to fight with me. He was very strong!

After a few minutes of true combat, fighting and wrestling with him, I succeeded in shoving him back into the enclosure, and pushed the entrance door shut, securing it with a pine branch.

Then I fell down and lost consciousness.

After some time, I awoke, and everything seemed very quiet and peaceful, except for the clicking sound of cicadas. I tried to stand up, but I collapsed again as I was quite dizzy.

I think I lost consciousness again for some minutes, and when I awoke it reminded me of the last war I was in, except there were no shots, just the clicking of the cicadas.

I saw that I was full of blood, which was still streaming from my back and left leg.

Unfortunately, I was alone in the reserve, as I had sent the ranger off in the Jeep to get some concentrated food for the animals.

I still felt extremely dizzy, and I couldn't find my cell phone.

After several minutes of searching, I found my cell phone on the ground several feet from where I was, under the old carob tree. But I couldn't remember any of the numbers of any of my colleagues!

I tried to call my son's clinic, which wasn't too far away from the Reserve, but I couldn't remember his number either.

Somehow I remembered the number of another ranger. I succeeded in reaching him, and he rushed to the Hai-Bar and took me in his vehicle, half-conscious, to the nearest hospital where I was treated in the emergency room.

There was a big hole in one of the blood vessels in my leg, and if I hadn't fallen in a certain way, with my knee bent back, I would not have survived.

I spent a number of days in the hospital and received several transfusions to get my blood level back to normal.

Since then, whenever I came back to the Nature Reserve to work, if I would walk anywhere near the enclosure, Albert was waiting to stab me.

One reason he attacked me was probably because he was "imprinted" on man (raised by humans), and thus saw me as a rival.

But, even now, many years later, the negative interaction between us hasn't ended. He still runs to the fence to try to get at me every time I come there.

So although we are both older, Albert's rivalry still remains.

And, like a dominant male, I understand these things.

Take A Monkey To Save A Baby!

When I was the young director of the Haifa zoo, our monkeys were a major attraction for the public because they were very energetic and funny—and people really enjoyed watching them.

One morning, as I was making my rounds to check the animals, I noticed that a young woman—a very pregnant young woman—was following me wherever I went.

She followed me for quite a while.

Finally, I asked her, "Dear lady, can I help you with anything?"

She didn't answer me right away. I saw that she was trying to find the right words, and she wasn't feeling at ease. It was also apparent that she had not come to the zoo to see the animals.

When she saw that I was sincerely interested in her story, she said:

"Look, I live in downtown Haifa. My husband is a sailor who loves me very much. He brought me a young monkey from Africa, which is very cute, but quite sad."

"I feed him and pet him," she continued, "but it's not easy to keep him in my small apartment, and we live with my mother who doesn't like him very much."

"In fact", she went on, "my mother told me if I look at the monkey too often, the baby that I'm expecting will look like a monkey."

I thought for a moment and decided right away that this was not the ideal situation for a monkey—and, because I wanted more monkeys for the zoo, my quick (and not so innocent) answer was, "I've heard about these cases, and I can't deny what your mother says."

Then she said, "Take the monkey. I don't want the monkey. I might have my baby any day."

I didn't feel good about this. I had influenced her decision unfairly, although, I believed, for the sake of the monkey's health, he should be taken from where he was.

"I will come in the evening after work to take the monkey," I told her. And when I got there that evening, I found a very small, rundown apartment with a huge container of couscous, some eggplant, and some unidentified sauce on the table.

I saw that a very small mustached monkey (a species which is not so common) was tied by a short cord to the legs of an armchair. He was very dirty and it seemed to me that he had some stomach problems. (When I saw the kind of food they had, I understood why).

I told the woman that I'd give her a permanent entry pass to the zoo so she could always come and visit her monkey, and that we'd be happy to accept her eight-year old son into our youth zoology club, and maybe he could grow up to be a zookeeper.

Then I took the monkey under my warm jacket and went home quickly because he needed special treatment, different food, and some veterinary checks. (I was not aware in those days that monkeys can also transfer a variety of diseases to man).

When I got home to my warm living room, my daughter, who was about two years old at the time, was lying in her bed with a bottle of cocoa in her hands.

The monkey didn't think twice. He jumped on her bed, took the cocoa, and drank half of it quickly. My daughter began to cry and we had to give her a new bottle.

After the monkey warmed up with the cocoa, he jumped all over the room, grabbed a handful of books from the bookshelf and threw them down. Then he took two precious vases my mother had given me and threw them down. Then he had diarrhea attacks all over the room because his stomach was out of order.

When I tried to catch him, he jumped and caught the chandelier and began to swing from it.

My wife didn't say anything, but her look was one of those dangerous looks that she gives me—more often than I'd like!!

I had to take the monkey out of the room because the room was now stinking and filthy, and I had to keep him somewhere until morning when I could take him to the zoo.

The best place I could think of to put him was the toilet room. (Many homes in Israel have a toilet room separate from the room with the sink and shower). After a short time, he found the way to pull on the chain of the water closet and he probably liked that action a lot, for he did it over and over, so I tied it with a piece of rope, and then it got very quiet.

My daughter, two sons, and wife went to sleep.

Feeling quite tired and filthy myself by then, I decided to take a shower and go to bed.

First, though, I thought I should peek into the toilet room. I opened the door a crack—and a wave of "noodles" of shredded toilet paper flew out! He had torn several rolls of toilet paper into pieces, which spread throughout the house!

The next morning, I got up very early, cleaned up the mess, took him to the zoo, and put him in a cage with an old Macaque female. He instinctively went to her, she hugged him, and I was very happy for both of them. She acted as his "foster mother" for quite a time, even while we continued to give him special milk through the cage bars until he was able to eat independently.

When I would visit, he would always jump back and forth from me to his foster mother, as if he couldn't decide which one of us to choose. The formerly-pregnant woman called me a few weeks later, inviting me to see her new baby. I went there. He appeared to be a nice, normal baby, and I observed that he didn't look like a monkey at all.

But she never visited the zoo again.

After a very long time, we found a mustached female for the little mustached monkey. They lived together for quite a while, but did not have any children.

Perhaps it was my imagination, but I still remember that this little monkey's eyes were always very very sad.

28

The Tiger Who Never Forgave Me

The current law in Israel is against keeping wild animals from wild sources in captivity, and it is especially against the law for people to keep them at home.

Wild animals can be kept only at zoos and at large animal corners because we don't want them to suffer. In private homes there are too many cases of neglect and improper treatment; and, in general, wild animals shouldn't be used for entertainment anyway.

It is also against the law in Israel now for circuses to use wild animals in their acts.

But, long ago, when I was director of the Wild Animal Protection Branch of the Nature Reserve Authority, a popular Italian circus played in Tel Aviv, using tigers as part of the show.

A few weeks after the circus went back to Italy, I got a tip from an animal lover that a well-known family in an Arab village had some tigers in their house—which was against the law—and that the tigers were not in good health.

Since this was a delicate matter and I was afraid that something might happen to the tigers if we went there with a fleet of cars and a lot of rangers, I decided to handle it in a "friendly way."

I drove to the village in my own car (instead of a Nature Reserve Jeep), knocked at the door, identified myself, and told the owner, "I came to help you take care of the sick tigers."

He invited me in and we sat in his living room with a lot of bitter Arab coffee and some very high quality sweets. He told me he had received three tiger cubs as partial payment for services and odd jobs he had done for the circus and they didn't have enough money to actually pay him.

The Arab man told me he had thought of building a small zoological garden for his community, but, after a few weeks, when the cubs got quite sick, he realized this might not be such a good idea, so he decided to let me take care of the tigers for a while.

I told him that since he was so cooperative, I would not cite him for keeping wild animals without a permit. I also told him I hoped he would get the money the circus owed him by other means.

And so we finished, "very friendly."

I looked at the three young tigers, which were about a month old, each the size of a small Chihuahua. They had diarrhea and were not clean, and two of them were very warm, probably with a fever.

I put them in a box with a lot of soft rags that I had brought for that purpose, and covered the box. The cubs were very quiet.

I put the box on the back seat of my car, thanked the guy, and began driving toward home (in Haifa).

A few miles after I left the Arab village, I picked up a tired and dusty soldier raising his hand to hitchhike and get a ride home (very common in Israel), as it was the end of the week.

I opened the front door on the passenger side, he got in, and was sound asleep in a few seconds, with very loud snores, as he was probably very tired.

As I approached a small town, the car in front of me stopped abruptly, and I had to stop fast.

When I hit the brakes, the whole box with the tiger cubs flew into the front of the car, and two of the tigers landed on the sleeping soldier, one on his shoulder and one on his leg.

He woke up suddenly, looked at me with wide eyes, opened his mouth to say something, but nothing came out—and, just as abruptly, he opened the car door without a word, and jumped out. I saw that he fell and rolled, in a cloud of dust. Then he got up and walked away with one hand pointing to his head to indicate that I was crazy.

When I got home an hour later, I first had to explain to my wife why my clothes smelled so bad. (As I was putting the tiger cubs back into the box in the car, they had diarrhea attacks, dripping all over me).

After very intensive vet treatment including antibiotics, special shots, and emergency special care, the little tigers came back to life. I fed them a very special mixture of goat's milk and other components, and treated their diarrhea until it stabilized.

The tiger cubs weren't easy to care for. First, it was pretty messy. Second, they ate a hole in a very expensive Persian carpet that my wife's mother had given us as a present.

Nevertheless, my wife and children enjoyed playing with them, and the tiger cubs enjoyed sleeping in my children's beds.

Two of the tigers were always together and slept with my young daughter, who was then about eleven years old; and one stayed with my elder son who played with him, teased him, took care of him, and became the "alpha male" for the little tiger.

We had the cubs for a few weeks until I transferred them out (because the house was a mess), putting two of them at two large "animal schoolyards" which had the right facilities for them; and I gave the third one to the Haifa Zoo.

The tiger at the Haifa Zoo grew very quickly, and, in the following months, I would visit him a few times a week.

The zoo people wanted to give him a better cage, and they didn't have funds, but they got a donation from a generous, old animal lover who always supported us "with open hands" because she wanted to prevent animals from suffering.

They built a very nice cage for this tiger, so it had room to walk around. It had a small pool and toys, and even a heated room for the winter.

The tiger and I were quite good friends.

Or so I thought.

When he was about ten months old, I entered his enclosure to play with him, as I did regularly. But this time the "play" (from his point of view) was extremely aggressive.

Suddenly, I found my left arm in his mouth with his teeth clamped down very tightly. (Tigers have very big, very long, very sharp teeth and strong jaws capable of exerting a lot of pressure).

He was applying a lot of force, blood was coming from the wound, and he wouldn't let go.

The natural response would be to try to pull your arm out.

I don't know how I managed NOT to do this, because he began to growl like a full-grown tiger, his hair began to stand on end, and he was getting very agitated.

A keeper who was watching from outside the cage ran to get a gun, and, although the pain was very strong, I adopted a calm, quiet approach.

I began to growl in a low voice, and pet the tiger to distract him—and he began to relax.

It took me quite a while to get my arm out of his mouth, very slowly, and there was a lot of (my) blood on the ground, but I finally managed to get out of the cage.

As soon as I was out of the cage, I nearly lost consciousness from the loss of blood, but I remember seeing him lick the blood from the floor of his cage—and he seemed to like it.

The keepers rushed over and gave me a lot of water, part of it poured on my head and part of it on my wound.

They wanted to take me directly to the hospital, but I went to the emergency room for some stitches and stayed home for a day to rest.

And that was the last time I entered the cage of this tiger—but not the end of the story...

A year later, they had to transfer the tiger to a larger enclosure.

They asked me to use my special animal gun to immobilize him so we could move him.

My mistake was that I was not hiding well when I shot him with the immobilizing gun, and he saw me.

Since then, whenever I'd get near the cage, the tiger would run toward me trying to push through the bars to claw and bite me.

I forgave him, but even two years after that, when I came to visit him at the zoo, he still tried to get at me—and complete what he felt was unfinished business between us.

Although I tried to be very low to the ground and soothe him and speak in a very soft voice and not meet eyes with him, he never forgave me.

Don't Ask a Wild Sand Cat to Be Your Babysitter

If we have to invent a cute animal, we wouldn't be able to find a better example than the sand cat. This animal is comparatively rare, and now probably extinct in Israel, as the last attempt to reintroduce them failed.

Possibly the smallest wild cat in the world, the sand cat is found in the hottest places on earth—north African deserts, the Sinai Peninsula, parts of the Arab Peninsula, and some parts of southern Jordan. They inhabit areas where the terrain is composed of moving, soft sand. Very few animals can live in areas where this type of sand exists because it shifts under your feet, the ground is not stable, and you just sink into the soft sand.

The sand cat has an advantage because it is very small, weighing little more than two pounds; and, more important, their paws have a lot of hairs that make the sand cat "float" on top of the fine sand, while larger wild cats can't walk or run on this kind of ground, so there are nearly no competitors or enemies for the sand cat.

In Israel, the sand cat was found in the extreme southern Part the Negev, north of Eilat, near the Hai-Bar South Nature Reserve, where the sand they thrive in was found.

Sand cats dig dens in comparatively stable ground and live underground in dark, comparatively cool dens, being most active at night or early in the morning before it gets hot.

Their prey is composed mostly of insects, small reptiles, birds, and special kinds of rodents that can survive in the same habitat, such as gerbils, kangaroo rats, and mice.

We knew that there were some specimens of this cat, albeit not many, at the extreme southern part of Israel, and, as we wanted to know more about their home range and ecology, we initiated a radio-tracking project.

The local ranger who initiated the project succeeded in catching and radio-collaring some specimens and he even found an active den where he located two kittens. He took one of the kittens, intending to radio-collar him later, and also to use for a possible breeding nucleus.

So he brought the little sand cat home; and since the sand cat was very young, they fed him with a special formula of milk until he became more independent and ate regular cat food.

The sand cat lived in their home like a normal "house" cat, behaving like a domestic cat, only it was very shy, and was more active during the night.

At the same time, the researcher's wife delivered their first child, and, as the house was very small, cat and baby were living in the same house.

One day the couple went to visit their neighbors who lived quite close by. The new parents had a speaker system to listen to their child while they were gone.

After a light supper at the neighbors', they suddenly heard loud crying from the baby.

They raced home and were astonished to find torn clothes and diapers and many deep scratches on the baby, obviously done by the sand cat.

They rushed the baby to the hospital, and he is now a perfect young boy, with a very few small scars.

They transferred the sand cat to a nice enclosure at the Hai Bar South nature reserve, and it was later used as part of a breeding pair of this very interesting species.

The simple message is that wild animals are wild. We never really have enough knowledge of the behavior and instincts of wild animals, so we shouldn't be surprised when they act normally, according to their instincts.

A Bear in My Bed &
A Jackal in My Oven

A (Syrian) Bear in My Bed

When I was director of the Haifa Zoo, one of my assistants was responsible for a female Syrian bear that was about to give birth. We isolated her in a warm room, and when the assistant was certain he heard the sounds of a newborn baby bear, he called me.

Actually, two Syrian bear babies were born, but after three weeks, my assistant came to me, quite concerned, and said:

"Something very strange is happening. The mother is only taking care of one of the babies, and the other one is lying and crying near the door of the room. She doesn't give it any milk, she doesn't take care of it, and the baby is getting weaker and weaker."

After long thought and some consulting with colleagues, I succeeded in getting the baby bear away from the mother by giving her some special honey bait on the other side of her room. Then I sneaked in and stole the few-week-old youngster, which was then about the size of a small cat.

I didn't ask the mother's permission, but I took the young bear to my home.

Actually, there was no other alternative (and my wife was very understanding, as usual).

We prepared a special diet as close as possible to the mother bear's milk, from a recipe we found in an old zoo yearbook.

The first night we put the bear in our home's shower room to sleep, with a warm blanket and a wall heater. After her supper, we turned off the lights and went to bed.

After a short time, the bear cub began to cry. We thought she would stop and go to sleep in a matter of minutes, so I gave her one of my daughter's dolls to hug. But the little Syrian bear continued to cry.

We couldn't sleep, so my wife said, "Let's take her into our bed."

So we put the little bear cub near our feet. She grabbed one of my socks from the floor to hold and suck (and ruin); and, like a child that comes into mommy and daddy's bed during the night, she fell asleep within seconds.

It was quite nice until morning came and we had to go to work, and I planned to take the little bear with me to the zoo for the day.

However, when I got up, I realized that the little bear had "done her duty" in our bed, and the smell and mess was quite bad.

So we changed our sheets and searched for a better solution.

We tried to put diapers on the little bear, but she would fiddle with them, they weren't tight enough, etc., and they just didn't work.

Then we found a solution: We put the bear to sleep near our dog.

But the little bear would still "do what comes naturally," which was quite a lot of work to clean up every day.

And, although we had her for several weeks, we "resigned" from this job at the first opportunity.

I found a proper home for her at the Biblical Zoo of Jerusalem, where they also had a young Syrian bear cub, and the two cubs became good friends.

About Syrian Bears:

At the beginning of the 20th Century, the last wild Syrian bears in Israel, an old female and her two cubs, were shot by hunters/collectors near Mt. Hermon in far north Israel, and their fur was sold.

The Syrian bear is a sub-species of, and a little different than the better-known European bear, and was quite common in

Syria in the 18th and 19th centuries. (One of the differences between the two is that the Syrian bear's claws are lighter in color).

In the 80s, I saw an army surveillance photo taken in Lebanon, and identified the animal in the photo as a Syrian bear.

It probably isn't possible to bring back Syrian bears to the wild in Israel any more because they couldn't survive for a variety of reasons: They would be a danger to people; there's not enough natural space; and there are not enough Syrian bears left in the world to take any from somewhere else.

So, although there may be a few Syrian bears still found in Iraq and Iran, the Syrian bear is close to global extinction.

Syrian bears are considered to be quite intelligent because they can learn lots of tricks and they were caught by people of the region because they were very good for shows and circuses—and this was also one of the reasons why they disappeared from this area.

As opposed to most animals, where you can see that they are angry or dangerous by their facial expression or their ear positions, the Syrian bear doesn't show any indication before it will "hit" you; and many people have been killed by not being aware of this.

We don't know if Syrian bears hibernate, but the females give birth to their young, in their dens, in the coldest part of winter, in January. The cubs then nurse and grow and are ready to eat the natural outdoor foods that will be available in the spring.

A Jackal in My Oven

It was one of those cold winter days in Israel. At that time, I was working as director of the Wild Animal Protection branch of the Nature Reserves Authority of Israel.

I was on my way to the Carmel Mountain area where we were planning to follow a Griffon vulture pair that had shown signs of looking for a nesting site—when I saw what looked like a dead jackal by the side of the road (a fairly common sight around this area).

But something caught my eye.

Although the animal appeared to be dead, I thought I saw a slight movement on the body.

So I stopped the car and went to check more closely to be sure this was really a jackal, as there were rumors that wolves were coming back to the Carmel after being absent for at least sixty years.

When I got closer, I saw that there were two young jackal puppies, one very stiff and dead, and the other huddled very close to the dead body of his mother for warmth; its tail moved slightly as a small sign of life.

Jackals, the coyote's cousin (and they look quite a bit alike), inhabit the Carmel in very large numbers as they have nearly no rivals or enemies. The behavior is nearly the same, they are from the same family, they are nearly the same size, and also the same opportunists; that is to say, they eat everything.

And, although jackals aren't considered cute, when I see a very young animal that is very weak and going to die, I can't ignore it. I'm sure that anybody would do the same thing for such a helpless creature.

I quickly picked up the tiny jackal and put her under my shirt (even though she was quite dirty); and I drove home as fast as I could.

Since it was Saturday (the Sabbath in Israel), everything in Haifa was closed.

My wife had gone to visit one of her sisters and the house was quite cold, so what should I do?

Sometimes, like a bolt of lightning, I get an idea. This time, I remembered that we had a kind of stove (oven) with a special Sabbath warmer that keeps food warm on a low heat on Shabbat (so religious people won't have to turn it on).

I turned on the Shabbat "switch," waited for the oven to warm, took the young jackal from under my shirt, put it in the oven, and went to my car to go and get special goat's milk and a combination of other ingredients (cream, egg yolk, glucose, etc.) that I thought would be a good recipe for "a little jackal's dinner."

I went to a small, nearby kibbutz, where they had a few goats. I milked one of them and went back home quickly—the milk was still warm.

When I opened the door to the house, my wife was standing there.

From the expression on her face, I knew that something "not positive" had happened.

"We can't go on like this!" she said. "I went to put some chicken in the oven, and when I opened the oven door, I heard a strange sound, a whimper—and then I saw a creature's head moving—and then a yelp, and then I nearly fainted."

"I couldn't understand what was happening", she went on. "I thought I was having a bad dream."

"Tell me," she demanded, "why is there an (unpleasant) animal in my oven!!??"

I hugged her and told her the whole story, and, because we didn't have cell phones at that time, I couldn't call and warn her; and I told her I was in a hurry to get the milk because the animal was in very bad condition.

And I think she understood—especially since this was not the first time I had done something strange like this (and also because I offered to clean the dishes for a whole week).

So, after comforting my wife and explaining everything, I quickly prepared the mixture, warmed it, and fed the jackal, using my daughter's doll bottle (which was just the right size).

For the next few days, I took the little jackal with me under my shirt wherever I went—and, after a couple of days of feeding it four times day and night—I gave it to a veterinarian friend to continue.

The little jackal survived and was later transferred to the local zoo.

It seems a flaw of mine to think about animals before I think about the results of what I do. Fortunately, I was smart enough to marry someone who has usually been very understanding and affectionate, regardless of my flaws.

The jackal I saved, on the other hand, didn't show any affection or gratitude at all—which is typical of jackals. He never became a good friend—which, I believe, is typical of some people, too.

My Leech Experiment

When I was a very young child in Jerusalem, about age eight, I lived with my grandfather (my mother's father) and he was one of my best friends.

I can picture him now, once every month, sitting on a big chair reading a newspaper, two leeches attached just behind his ears, almost on his throat, and snapping a whip.

I was fascinated by how fast the leeches were getting larger and larger, and, after a while, they fell down on a newspaper on the floor beside the chair.

He would put the leeches back into a big jar of water, and then he would give a big sigh, a satisfied groan—a positive sound that he had enjoyed himself.

Many years later, I was sitting in my office at the Nature Reserves Authority (in Jerusalem), thinking about building a new salamander pond in the Carmel Hai-Bar Nature Reserve, when there was a knock at my door, and a short man, wearing very heavy glasses, entered.

He sat down in front of me, and said, "I need your help."

I must admit that this sentence always attracts my attention.

"Look," he said, "I'm a doctor at a well-known hospital in Jerusalem. I have a patient, not a young one, who had an operation on her leg, and the wound is now full of necrotic (dying) tissues, and," he continued, "although we tried intensive antibiotics and other means of care, we can't control it and we are thinking of amputation."

"When I was a young student at an Eastern European university," he went on, "we used local leeches quite extensively for a variety of diseases. And, even though my boss at the hospital is against it, I want to try it anyway, because we have

45

nothing to lose. The only problem," he said, "is that I don't know how to get leeches here." (The Latin name for these leeches is: *Hirudo medicinalis*, the European medical leech).

I told him that since I knew the Israeli fauna quite well, I was aware of at least one place in the Golan Heights where there was a clean water source, and you could still find some leeches there.

After about two weeks, I succeeded in (secretly) getting about six leeches from the special place. I gave the leeches to the doctor and forgot about the whole story.

About three months later, he came back into my office without knocking, and, grinning, he showed me a few photos.

"Look at her legs before and after," he said, adding, "I'm sorry, but I can give you only three leeches back—the others died. And, by the way," he added, "the woman is back walking on her own legs!"

"You'd think that one of my colleagues would have said, 'thank you,'" he said, "but they didn't. That's ok."

And then he left.

For some reason, maybe because I am not completely normal, I decided that I wanted very much to feel what my grandfather felt.

So I took two of the leeches in my office and tried to put them on my skin. I tried to put them on my throat, on my chest, on my hands—but they wouldn't attach.

Finally, one of them got attached to my throat, below my chin, just below the jaw bone...

I felt a very short burning sensation and I continued to write a few words, when my secretary entered the room. After she uttered a few sentences, her eyes got wide, she pointed at my throat, and then she fainted.

I rose and helped her, and she pointed again without saying anything.

"It is just a leech," I told her, and she came back to her senses, and left the room, mumbling something about my "abnormality."

I began to feel a little nervous because it was taking the leech quite a long time to finish her "dinner" and she wouldn't let go of my body.

So I went into the toilet and pulled the leech off and put it in the jar—and then... the blood began to flow from where the leech had been attached.

I used my hand to try to stop the bleeding.

I tried several times to take my hand off, but the blood was still flowing.

It was quite late when I decided to drive back home to Haifa (my office was in Jerusalem), and, as I had to use one hand to press on my open wound with a piece of cotton, I had to drive with the other hand.

Halfway to Tel Aviv, I felt quite tired, and decided to stop at the Tel Aviv home of my good friend and teacher, Prof. Mendelssohn, who was then considered to be the guru of all zoologists.

When I entered his room, with one hand pressing my wound, he asked me, "What's the matter, Avi?" And when I told him, he said. "Keep the hand pressed, I'm going to take care of you."

Then he went and took from his cupboard a small amount of Arabic coffee with some cardamom in it, approached me, and put a whole handful of the coffee on my wound, pressing it for a minute or two.

When he took his hand off, the bleeding had stopped, and he was very happy, and said, "It is something I learned from an old Arab Sheikh."

When I got home later that day with my shirt full of blood and coffee stains, my wife was sure I had been in the middle of a very bloody fight.

Since then, however, I have come to like leeches very much.

You see, I have always admired unsympathetic creatures— especially one that has to be very patient until someone comes along to provide something for her to eat.

Boars at Your Doors?

More and more these days, I receive calls from friends or acquaintances to tell me that they have seen wild boars outside the doors of their building, or in their yards, or on the road—and they ask my advice about what to do.

Some people are delighted and call the neighbors to "come and see the safari" when this happens; other people call the police and tell them that "monsters" are entering their yard.

Wild boars are one of the largest wild mammals in Israel now. They are not close to extinction. In fact, they are overpopulated, as they reproduce rapidly and they have no natural enemy. Their former natural enemy, the leopard, is now extinct from the north and central part of Israel; and the number of wolves is now too small to affect the boar population.

Wild boars are very strong. If they are cornered they will protect themselves; and they have killed a number of hunters' dogs.

These days the boars' main enemy is the common hunter, although some people say that both have nearly the same intelligence. (I confess that I was not authorized to check this). Boar hunting season in Israel normally runs from September to the end of January, but boars that cause agricultural damage can be hunted at any time with a special permit. Otherwise there is no way to balance their population size.

A long time ago, boars used to be active during the daytime, but due to increased human activity and danger from hunters, boars became nocturnal. Actually, there is still at least one place where you can see boars active during the day. That's in the area where the borders of Jordan, Israel, and Syria meet. Because of the strict military restrictions, there is nearly no human activity there, so you can watch the boars walking around during the day in a relaxed mode—if you can get to this location.

Nobody knows how many boars there are now in Israel, but they are now seen very often during the night if they are under pressure to find food or water. Their need for food and water is stronger than their fear of people; and, as there are not many hunters, the boars are just not afraid.

The wild boar is an interesting opportunist. Like us, he eats everything, although he prefers meat (protein). The wild boar's social structure is that there are groups of females with young, and the males are connected to the females mostly only in the breeding season.

The female is a very devoted mother, giving birth to up to nine young ones. When they are born, they have light-colored, long stripes along their body. An orphaned young wild boar can easily imprint on humans.

The boars' main problem in Israel is that this country is comparatively dry and there are very few water sources. In recent years, at the end of the summer when there was no water source at their hiding places, the boars would be found in big cities, along wide roads, entering gardens and meadows with grass; in yards, where they eat plants with bulbs; and they also try to dig for fresh roots, earthworms, and whatever they can find in a common garden.

So boars are quite a problem at the end of every summer, especially in the northern part of the country; and every year they are more daring.

The mothers take care of their young until the following breeding season (one year), and during that time she teaches them when to eat, where to eat, and what to eat; and she even teaches them how to identify the enemy (the hunter).

I believe the scenario goes something like this: In the evening, the mother boar, with her children, conducts a reconnaissance of a corn or alfalfa field, the potential dinner, which they like very much... but her senses are quite sharp and she smells, even from a distance, the hunter waiting for them.

She tells her children, "Look, my child, the hunter is sitting at the top of the third pine tree not too far from us... Can you smell that? He is now smoking a cigarette... oh, do you hear that noise? He is just taking a sandwich from his bag and crinkling the paper... but wait... around 9 pm he is going home to watch a compelling telenovella (soap opera)... and he will leave with his green Jeep which stands behind the big tree... and THEN we can quietly enter the field and have a nice feast."

I still remember what one kibbutz secretary told me some years ago when the boars were doing a lot of damage to their banana plantation; he thought he might do something different than using hunters, who are sometimes not very active and are tired, and don't do the job very well...

So, one evening, at one of the kibbutzim, he asked all the people who came to supper to take their shoes off—I understand the smell was awful. He collected all their stinky socks, put them in a big plastic bag, took his vehicle, and hung all the stinking socks around the banana plantation, with clothespins.

To the amazement of the kibbutz people, not even one boar dared to enter the banana plantation for several weeks. Then the bananas became ripe, and one, (probably especially intelligent male) dared to enter the plantation and saw that there was nobody there; only dirty socks; and he ran to tell his friends, "come and have nice food"... but, by then most of the ripe bananas had already been taken to the market. And ever since then, this method was no longer effective.

Other ways of distracting the boars included putting a portable radio that played noisy music all day and all night to make the boars believe there were people there, so they wouldn't come; but, after a short time, the boars got used to this, too.

The only effective way to prevent the boars from entering agricultural places ultimately was to build a very special, cleverly-designed strong fence to protect the plantation. (It doesn't have to be very high as boars' jumping ability is limited).

Another "method" was that some hunters would make a feeding station of chicken heads (which boars like very much), and, after the boars would get used to eating there, the hunters would put special chemicals in the food (which is illegal); and many of the boars would fall asleep near the feeding station, and the hunters would then come and shoot them when they were asleep.

As the chemical remained in the boars' blood, the owner of a leading restaurant told me, in a few cases it happened that people in his restaurant ordered and enjoyed some wild boar steaks, then fell asleep at the table from the effect of the sleeping potion given to the boars, whose meat was unknowingly bought and served at the restaurant!

Future horror dream: As I said that wild boars are quite intelligent, I am afraid of the day when they might learn how to use computers!

Vulture Love Stories

Part One: Late Love

Both lived in the heights of the Carmel Mountain.

He was seven years old (about the equivalent of an 18-year-old in vulture age); and she was a nice grandmother, over thirty years old.

He was flying freely between the Carmel Mountains and the Golan Heights.

She was living in a large cage at the Carmel Hai-Bar Reserve with six young vultures that were going to be released after being fitted with electronic transmitters to track them for the next three years of the transmitters' battery life.

(Vultures went extinct from the Carmel region of Israel in the mid 1950s, so we hoped that the young vultures we released from the enclosure in the Carmel Hai-Bar in recent years would be inspired to stay in the Carmel area, once a very popular vulture-nesting site).

I don't remember when this unusual relationship started...

But one day we observed among the free-flying vultures who frequently visited the cage, that young vulture—about seven years old according to his leg ring—who started an interesting love affair with this old female.

They would look into each other's eyes—she in the cage, he outside the cage. They even had contact through the cage mesh—he would play with her feathers, and she would play with his.

The cage was built on a rocky slope that ran from outside the cage through the cage—and the vultures would build nests on it.

One day I noticed that he brought her a little branch and gave it to her through the mesh of the cage. (He usually did this when there were no visitors around). She took the present and petted his feathers with her beak (a sign of happiness).

And then they began to build a nest together. Part of it was inside the cage, and part of it was outside the cage, and it grew bigger every day.

Although it was cold winter, both of them were very active builders. Love was flourishing, and the looks between them, without words, said everything.

Until today, I don't know exactly why, but I decided to let her out of the cage to be closer to her young lover. Maybe I was too romantic. But, very gently, I put her on the cage roof. It seemed that he read my thoughts, for he just stood near her, and they loved as only vultures can love. During this time, they added hardly anything to the nest.

After two days, he opened his wings and flew and made a few pirouettes over the nice *wadi* (valley) that the cage overlooked. She wanted very much to join him and to get to the high cliffs which she always loved and used to frequent in the past, a very popular nesting site. But her muscles were weak and she didn't have enough power; so, after a very short flight, she landed, very tired, on the side of the hill.

He continued to fly, and he invited her to join him for lunch at the feeding station on the facing hillside, not too far away.

She tried to take off and glide, but with no success, and she just fell to the ground.

Days passed. We knew she was hungry, but our attempts to catch her didn't succeed, as she always would fly several yards out of reach when we approached her.

After several days, very tired, she ended up on the main street of a small town nearby, where we were called by the local nature-lover policeman. When we rushed there, we recognized her immediately. We put a blanket over her and returned her to the cage, wounded, full of thorns, and very thirsty.

At the cage, she rested and calmed down, and went back to caring for the nest that they had been building.

She waited for him in the cage, but he didn't come.

Where could he be?

Two weeks later, he appeared again, and stood on the roof of the cage where she was living.

But this time he was not alone. With him was another vulture, young; we believe it was a wild female, as she had no ring or transmitter—and they were both flying around outside the cage, later disappearing into the horizon.

It was clear that he preferred his younger mate, and he didn't pay any attention to his old girlfriend.

After a few days, the older woman got desperate and stopped eating and retreated to the back of the cage. Her head just fell between her wings where she huddled in the dark corner. More days passed, and she became weak and forlorn, and we were quite worried...

After consulting with several specialists and nature lovers, we found, in one of the zoos in the central part of the country, a lonely male that had a wounded wing and couldn't fly any more.

The meeting between them began with indifference, and they didn't pay any attention to each other. But, as time passed, she got back her appetite and he probably discovered her good heart; and love began to flourish again.

Although they didn't build any nest, they would just stand together—and it would seem to the visitor that they loved each other... She returned to her normal routine and I think they are still living together happily.

In my last visit there, I stood, excited at the sight of the happy pair, looking into each other's eyes lovingly, enjoying the beautiful spring day.

(And the young male? A year after flying away, the young male and female were known to be nesting in the Golan Heights, and had their first chick).

54

Part Two: an Uncommon Love Story: "Gay" Vulture Couple Goes Straight

About ten years ago, there were two very good friends in a special cage at the Biblical Zoo in Jerusalem.

Dashik and Yehuda were both males, and, despite a lot of prospective matches, they didn't want to build nests or form any close relations with any female offered to them.

But they behaved like a couple with each other! They would touch each other's feathers, and they would stand very close to each other.

A few years later, an egg was sent from the Hai-Bar Carmel to be incubated at the sophisticated facilities of the zoo; but, before putting it into an incubator, they put it into the cage of the two males for a few hours; and, quite suddenly, the two began to actively collect materials in their cage and build a nest.

After being given more materials, a beautiful nest was completed and the guys sat on the egg for more than fifty days.

A chick hatched—and they treated it with great care—a beautiful female named Carmela, she was later brought to the release cage at the Carmel Hai-Bar Nature Reserve.

After a few more years, the love story between Dashik and Yehuda collapsed, and each of them accepted females who laid eggs and produced more chicks—and the two guys continue to behave like normal male vultures to this day.

Whitey the Rooster

During and after the War of Independence, it was difficult to get fresh food, or food at all for that matter. We had some fruits and vegetables growing around our house in Beit HaKerem. We also had a small chicken coop with a few chickens that supplied us with fresh eggs. Of course, many neighbors were envious because nobody else had things like this during the blockade of Jerusalem.

Among the few, colorful chickens that we had, there was one specific white rooster that my father had bought for me in the market, and I had raised it from a chick to become a very nice adult.

Early one morning, when I was about ten years old, I heard cries of distress from the chickens, so I grabbed my air rifle and ran to the coop. As I approached, I saw a jackal with my favorite white rooster in its mouth, and all the other chickens were clucking hysterically.

I instinctively aimed my gun at the jackal and shot once. He dropped the cock, which lay there stiff and unmoving, and ran away.

I ran after the jackal—and half an hour later I found his dead body about two hundred yards from my house. He had blood just below his left eye, and I understood that the bullet had penetrated his brain and it was a quick death.

When I came back to the yard, I saw one of the rooster's legs moving, so I turned him over and petted him. And then, first one eye opened, and then he was able to stand on both his legs; but as a result of the attack, he had permanent wounds on one of his legs and on his throat. The worst thing was that his vocal cords were also injured and, even though he tried, he was never able to crow again.

I was so happy that my friend Whitey survived the jackal's attack.

Two years after the war, when it was still difficult to get meat, and there was food rationing, we had a very nice dinner on one of the holidays, with my aunt and uncle and grandfather.

My mother brought out a beautiful, golden-roasted chicken and set it in the middle of the table.

As the young male child, my mother picked out the best part of the chicken for me, a part that all children love, and she put it on my plate.

I looked down at the chicken drumstick, which still had the skin on it, and I immediately noticed something familiar—the old scar in a certain shape that had remained on Whitey's leg after the jackal attacked it.

I cried out to my mother to come from the kitchen, and demanded: "Is this our Whitey? Did you kill him? Why? How could you do this? How can we eat him?"

I will always remember her reaction of complete surprise when I asked—and she refused to admit anything.

I immediately left everybody sitting at the table, ran to my room, and put a big chair against the door so nobody could come in.

I couldn't believe that this happened to me and my Whitey! I felt especially bad because I believed this was breaking a trust that we had. Maybe also, because there was no meat in those days, except in the black market, my mother may have thought that her skinny son needed some meat in his diet, and decided it was better to sacrifice the chicken than her son's health.

Even many years later, it bothered me that she still wouldn't admit anything or say she was sorry.

And, as I think about it now, I STILL don't feel very good. I couldn't understand it then, and I probably still don't. It was such a big disappointment in my life. Maybe that's why I became a vegetarian for quite a long time after that, and why my stomach still turns when I am served chicken.

This was probably the beginning of learning to cope with unpleasant things in my life. The moral may be: You can save a chicken from a jackal, but not from your mother's oven!

The Case of the Missing Pecans

There were no pecans in Israel when I was young, although the king nut (walnut) was very common. Nowadays, pecan-growing is a very popular agricultural industry in Israel, with many pecan plantations in the central and northern parts of the country.

However, in the 1980s, a very strange phenomenon began to occur as the industry began to grow: The ripe pecans were disappearing just before the time of picking them and we couldn't understand why. Farmers were sustaining huge losses and were very upset; they wanted to get to the bottom of the problem.

Pecans were such a desirable item, there were rumors that gangs of thieves were coming during the night, picking the pecans in large quantities, and selling them on the black market.

Also, about that time, there were many conflicts between farmers and animal "protectors"—so some wild animal populations had gotten quite out of balance, growing to large numbers, and were impinging on agriculture for their food sources.

One day, I was with another ranger, checking porcupine damage to a young avocado plantation, when we saw a strange-looking young guy in his late teens—very poor, tattered clothes, matted hair, sandals made of cheap rubber from tires—with a heavy sack on his back, trying to walk toward his shabby, old, three-wheeled bicycle.

We suspected that the parcel he was carrying might contain stolen property.

So we approached the young man, with a policeman accompanying us, and asked him to open his sack.

We were certain that we had a big-time criminal. But he grinned, even with a few missing teeth, and, without any

59

problem, opened his sack, and we saw that it was full of pecan nuts.

"Where did you buy these? Do you have a receipt?" we asked him.

"I wouldn't buy these nuts; they're too expensive for me," he answered. "I found them in a distant field not far from Binyamina."

We got very excited that we had found one of the culprits in a pecan-stealing crime ring.

Since we were quite sure he wasn't telling the truth, we said, "You told us you found them in a field—very interesting—will you come with us to that field and maybe we can find such things, too?"

We were grinning. We were certain he had stolen the nuts.

"No problem," he said, and we took him with us in our vehicle; and as we talked, I realized that I knew his family, and I had even drunk special Bedouin coffee at his uncle's tent.

About a half hour from the place where we stopped him, the young man directed us to a field. Before us was a huge, empty field, not used for anything, full of stones and all kind of junk, and he said, "This is the field."

I said (very smugly), "I don't see any pecans here."

"This is my secret," he replied, "but you have to assure me you won't tell anybody because this is my only income."

"We are civilized—and it will stay your secret—as long as it is legal," we responded.

He entered the field with us, took a few stones and tossed them aside, and, under nearly every stone, were several pecan nuts!

We thought this was just a coincidence, so we tried other parts of the field, and most of the field had pecans hidden under pieces of rock, wood, junk, etc.

And then, I knew!

This was a hiding place of the common crow. As this bird is well-known as one of the smartest thieves, (it takes shiny things, as well as all kind of fruits, or, actually, any edible food), I have to say that we are safe in calling the crow one of the best opportunists that there is.

So we looked at the young guy, very disappointed that we were wrong; we gave him an embarrassed grin, gave him back his pecans; stopped at a small kiosk on the way back to buy him a nice ice cream, and sent him on his way.

A little more about crows:

The common crow is considered an enemy of agriculture; it can peck holes in watermelons, damage all kinds of fruits, kill songbird chicks, and, of course, steal pecan nuts.

The common crow has no natural enemy because a group of them can frighten even a large bird of prey. There are even records of attacks on people who had picked up young crow chicks which had fallen out of their nests to the ground. When this happened, a group of crows would dive at the humans and peck and wound their heads and faces quite badly.

We didn't know how to control the crows because they were quite intelligent. (As a matter of fact, I once raised a very young chick who fell from the nest, and, after not so long a time, he could speak Hebrew with a sabra accent better than the best parrot)!

The crows were so smart, they could recognize the green Jeeps of the rangers coming; they knew the range of the shotguns; they flew just far enough away to avoid the danger, and they always returned to the place from which they flew when the spot was safe again.

We even tried to give them some poisons, which they identified after a very short time, and they succeeded to influence all the other crows not to touch the bait. So we had to change the bait—and, in the end, we had already lost—until we read in an Australian journal about some very interesting research—and this gave us the solution.

61

We learned from this article that, although the crow is very intelligent, he's still got one problem that is similar to humans: He doesn't like that someone else will enjoy something if he can't!

So we built a huge enclosure with a very special roof that had inward hooks so birds could get in, but not get out. The first time, we tried to put very attractive food inside, but after a very short time, they wouldn't go into this trap.

Then, to take advantage of the crows' personality, we put inside the cage a crow which we had raised, with a red ring on his leg to identify him: As the crows can't stand it if another crow has something and they don't, they are thinking, "if there's a crow inside, he shouldn't be allowed to eat alone," and they came into the cage in huge numbers.

And, since crows would normally be expected to go and roost in trees miles from the cage, we would come into the cage during the night, remove all the crows trapped inside, "send them to the Ministry of Agriculture for research," and the crows that came the next day wouldn't know that many of their brothers and sisters had disappeared.

The next morning, new crows would see the empty cage with the same crow with the red ring on his leg, surrounded by very special hard-boiled eggs and pieces of chickens, and they would come into the cage in large numbers because they couldn't stand to let this one crow eat alone.

Unfortunately, this was the only way to lower their numbers.

We believe that one day they will catch on to the secret, but just now it still works.

Rare People, Animals & Experiences

General Yoffe and My Work with the Nature Reserves

Gen. Avraham Yoffe was a well-known general in the Israeli Army—well-known for his skills and strategies in battle; for his propensity for fine food, wine and cheese; and also for hunting the animals of Israel—until he "found religion" and became a protector of nature, and the first head of Israel's Nature Reserves Authority in the early 60s.

As I have fought in all of Israel's wars, I knew about General Yoffe, but I don't think he knew about me.

One day, in late 1978, when I was the Director of the Haifa Zoo, he showed up at my office.

He introduced himself, because he didn't think I knew who he was, but I had seen his picture all over the newspapers and heard about his military exploits; I also knew that he had a good sense of humor.

A very large man, the first thing he said to me was, "Do you have a cage here for ME?"

"Should you be in one? Are you dangerous?" I answered back.

And then he said, "Look, I see on your table half a bottle of water and half a glass of tea, and I understand that this is a very poor zoo, so I'm going to take you to the Carmel Center (for something to eat) to make you larger—you are too skinny—and, besides, I want to talk to you."

I still had no idea what he wanted.

As he was well-known as the first director of the Nature Reserves Authority, I was worried. Why did he come to the

zoo? Maybe I didn't keep the wild animals in the right way?
Maybe there were some complaints?

I couldn't think of any reason for him to come, except that
maybe something was wrong.

So we went to one of the restaurants at the Carmel Center,
and he told me that he had heard a lot about me and about the
way I had saved the dying zoo.

And then he said, "The zoo doesn't need you any more—the
country needs you! We just succeeded in passing the law in the
Parliament for animal protection; we now have the authority to
do something. We have very few zoologists at the Nature
Reserves Authority and, to be brief, I want you to leave those
cages, come to work with us, and help get control of all the wild
animal problems in the country."

Some of the problems at that time were:

— A lot of local poachers liked to hunt partridge to make a
very special food; they also liked to hunt gazelles as they were
told it would enhance their prowess to have several women
every night.

— There were not enough rangers working for the Nature
Reserves Authority at the time. (Rangers were, and still are,
responsible for all kinds of problems connected to nature
preservation: They had to love animals; be able to differentiate
between all kinds of waterfowl; know what is protected and
what isn't; know the flowers, trees, and everything; and, perhaps
most important, be able to convince people to protect these
values.

— In addition, there were many conflicts between wild
animals and agriculture. For example, there was a lot of damage
being done by overly-large, unbalanced populations of wild
chukar partridge and wild boars, and also predation on livestock
by jackals.

— There were problems with people cutting rare trees to use
the wood for heating.

— There were problems with people picking and selling
huge amounts of colorful wildflowers.

66

— There was also the fact that, in general, the local population was not educated to obey the new hunting regulations and rules, that is to say, most people thought they could hunt whenever and wherever they wanted.

General Yoffe told me more about establishing The Nature Reserves Authority, which would be over all these things— protection, developing the Hai-Bar Nature Reserves, setting budgets for people to work at these places, the importance and plans for animal reintroductions to the country, and much more.

"I strongly suggest that you come to Tel Aviv next week," Gen. Yoffe said to me. "I want you to meet the leading staff and tell me the shortest time that it will take you before you will begin working with us."

Then we talked small talk and I discovered that we both had a hobby of collecting old books of zoology, and also old children's books. Of course his collection was much richer than mine, but we talked and talked for hours until he had to leave because he had a very important meeting with one of the cabinet ministers in Tel Aviv.

That was near the end of 1978, in September, and I began to work as Director of the Wildlife Conservation Department of the Israel Nature Reserves Authority in February, 1979.

That was also the beginning of extremely good relations between me and General Avraham Yoffe (whom I called "Avram").

Looking back, I believe I gained one or two kilograms of weight when he asked me to do the job, because I was so flattered.

There were other zoologists. Why did he choose me? I was comparatively young then. I think that he probably had heard about me from somebody. I never asked him why.

Yoffe was an amazingly witty, very clever man. He was very busy all his life with the army, with protecting the country, and one of the best soldiers we ever had. He had also been a free-wheeling hunter, shooting at everything—even, I'm told, stopping to shoot at something on the way to a battle campaign.

Then something happened to him. At the beginning of the 60s, something changed, and he became one of the most dedicated animal protectors we ever had!

Although he was not a zoologist, he was a quick study—he just learned by himself without any official school or university—and, as he was a hunter, he knew wild animals quite well.

I'm really happy I decided to accept his offer, because a new world opened to me about vast problems of animals in the wild; about new problems that I hadn't studied at the university (at least not enough); and I had a chance to be in many places in the country, and be involved with reintroduction and protection of the animals.

Gen. Yoffe sent a lot of guests and dignitaries to me, to show them around the Hai-Bar Nature Reserves, educate them about what we were doing, and explain to them, in my secondary school English, about animals, what they need, why it was important to reintroduce them, and help get donations for further development.

Speaking of donations, I said earlier, it was well-known and documented that not only was General Yoffe very charismatic, and that he loved fine food. One of his favorite lines was to say, jokingly, "Since I am a very large man, I am on a very large diet!"

But it was his attitude toward food that led to a very wonderful relationship with one of the best supporters of the Nature Reserves Authority we ever had.

Dolly

Her name was Dolly. She would walk around the Carmel Hai-Bar with her husband, looking at the wildflowers and the birds, and they would see our Druze ranger, Salach. She didn't know Arabic and he couldn't speak English, but their mutual love for nature and animals—and a good cup of Arabic coffee—somehow bridged this, and they became friends.

Salach introduced me to this lovely Dutch woman and her husband, Hank, and we all became very good friends, and I took her to other reserves, and eventually introduced her to Avraham Yoffe, who was anxious to meet her because he knew she wanted to help us.

She was born in England, and Avram's sense of humor just melded with her English sense of humor; their personalities meshed; and she really fell in love with him—and, he with her—and their friendship continued for a long time.

Whenever he had the time in his schedule, Avram would say to me, "Make a date with her at her home"—and she was always so happy to have us visit her, and we always ate a large variety of cheeses and fine foods there. He appreciated very much her selection of, may I say, "walking cheeses"—Roquefort, Romadur, and even Limburger—they were so ripe! She was a very creative cook, and I think that's the reason my cholesterol is so high today!

Dolly contributed large sums of money, with which we built the roads and enclosures of Hai-Bar Carmel. She also helped other reserves with support for educational projects. Whenever we needed something, she always had an "open hand."

Meeting with the hunting organization.

Another anecdote I remember about Gen. Yoffe was a meeting we had with the director of a hunter's organization.

The hunters wanted to hunt everywhere in the country all the year long. But we had limited the hunting season to just a few months; and of course limited only to animals that were not close to extinction; and of course not in the breeding season, and not to take more than the bag limit.

So the hunting organization's leader came to this meeting along with two or three other hunters. He was very defensive, and very uncomfortable, so when the waitress brought a few glasses of tea on a tray, the hunting leader took the first one and handed it to General Yoffe, saying, "You are older than me, so you will drink first."

General Yoffe looked into his eyes and said, "My dear guest, I am not only older, I am also MORE beautiful AND wiser than you! Didn't you notice???"

The guy was shocked; he couldn't see the humor in this, and he and the other hunters left the room in a huff, very offended, and without saying goodbye. This was the last personal meeting the hunters' organization had with us, even though we thought it was very funny and laughed about it for a long time after.

Let me quickly say, however, that hunters are essential to lower the dense populations of some species of wild animals that cause damage to the agriculture, as the whole ecosystem has lost its balance; and, as there is no natural enemy to many of these animals, the hunter is sometimes the best solution.

My wonderful relationship with Avram Yoffe ended at the beginning of the 80s, when he gave me a very special watch (I am a wristwatch collector) and a few books, just before he died.

Mesopotamian Fallow Deer: A Rare, Old Persian Citizen Returns to Israel

From many archaeological sites and old books, we knew that the Mesopotamian Fallow Deer were once quite common in Israel; and were even used as a popular food source by ancient, Carmelitic Man.

This beautiful deer was considered extinct from the world at the end of the 19th century, but they were rediscovered by a kind of miracle.

A German zoology student was studying wildlife in Iran in the mid 1950s, when, on the bank of the Dez River, not far from the Caspian Sea, he discovered strange hoof prints which he couldn't identify.

He made a gypsum mold and brought it to his professor at his university in Germany, and the professor surmised that these were made by the supposedly extinct Persian (Mesopotamian) fallow deer.

They approached the wealthy automobile producer, Baron von Opel, who agreed to finance a group of scientists to go back to Iran and make a more thorough search, with the result that two pair of Mesopotamian fallow deer were brought to the Von Opel Zoo near Frankfurt, Germany in the mid 50s.

How Israel got the deer

Here's the story of how Israel got a few Mesopotamian fallow deer to form the breeding nucleus that would lead to the largest herd of Mesopotamian fallow deer in the world:

In 1964, the Nature Reserves Authority in Israel was just getting off the ground and the first general director of the Nature Reserve Authority was Gen. Avraham Yoffe, a famous former hunter who became the most ardent animal protectionist.

When Gen. Yoffe heard that these rare Mesopotamian fallow deer had been found in Iran, he set his sights on finding a way to get these rare deer back to their homeland. Depending on your source, there are a few variations to the story.

My information is from personal sources that included Gen. Avraham Yoffe, head of Israel's Nature Reserve Authority at the time; Gen. Yitzhak Segev, who was the Israeli army attaché in Iran when this happened; Mike van Grevenbroek, the zoologist who captured the deer in Iran that were ultimately brought to Israel; Salach the Druze, who raised the deer when they were brought to Israel; and Uri Tzon, General Yoffe's assistant, who was part of the original idea of getting and bringing back the deer.

The Story

The story goes that the brother of the Shah of Iran, Prince Abdul Reza Pahlavi, was a very enthusiastic collector of horns and antlers and mounts of animals of the region.

He had a cousin who was also a collector. And, while the Shah's brother's collection was impressive, it did not include any Nubian ibex horns, while his cousin had a set of these horns that were nearly one meter long.

The Shah's brother apparently began to lose sleep over this—and sought a way to get ibex horns for his own collection that would be bigger than those his cousin had.

At that time, the Nubian ibex, which was on the edge of extinction at one time in Israel, began to increase in numbers because hunting them in the wild in Israel was nearly totally outlawed.

A Jewish photographer in Teheran named Firooz was also a hunter, and he told the Shah's brother about the Israeli ibex.

The Shah's brother secretly asked General Yoffe if he could come to Israel and hunt one big trophy male for his collection.

Normally, the answer would be, "no", but the shrewd Yoffe, knowing about the rediscovery of the Persian fallow deer, thought, "I'll get something more important in exchange for one old male ibex that is part of our revived fauna." And, although it was against the law to hunt for ibex, the law was bent in this very special case for this very special goal.

So early in 1979, the Shah's brother came to Israel incognito, but with quite a large entourage that included a cook, barber, tailor, taxidermist, sniper, etc.

A small group of Nature Reserve representatives and experts, including me, wandered all over southern Israel with the Shah's brother's delegation, searching for a suitable trophy. Using special binoculars to locate a proper male with horns that would be big enough, we failed to find one!

The last chance was to look at the nice ibex herd at the Hai-Bar Nature Reserve near Yotvata in far southern Israel. There, we found a very old male in the final phase of his life, with an estimated age of nearly twenty years; and he was not in good health; he just stood on a rock, and, after we estimated the horns to be quite large, the Shah's brother asked his special hunting assistant to shoot it.

The horns turned out to have a span of one meter, 25 centimeters, bigger than his cousin's trophy.

A day later, the Shah's brother and his whole delegation flew back to Iran, and he called Gen. Yoffe and said, "We got back safely, and, with special gratitude, I'm going to send you two Cadillacs as small thanks for your help in this matter."

According to his assistant, Uri Tzon, General Yoffe shivered when he heard this. "That's not what we wanted," Yoffe replied to his caller. "No, no, no, please," he said. "I have a very good Volvo. I don't need a Cadillac, and neither does my assistant."

"If possible," Yoffe continued, "we would like to get a pair of the new deer that were rediscovered in your country by the

Germans, and which were put at the fenced reserve at the place named Semeshkande" (not far from the Caspian Sea).

"Not a problem," came the reply. "You can have two pairs." And then the Shah's brother added, "Just send, as soon you can—somebody who knows animals—and we shall help him as much as we can."

For some reason, the follow-through to get the deer from Iran took longer than expected. The Shah's brother came to Israel around the end of 1978; Yoffe went to Iran to collect the deer, but suffered a minor heart attack when he was there and had to come home before he could complete the process.

Then, in early 1979, when the previously good relations between Iran and Israel were entering a different atmosphere in Iran, a daring plan was set into action. We sent one of our best animal keepers to Teheran, a Dutch guy by the name of Mike von Grevenbroek, who was blonde with blue eyes, didn't look like a typical Israeli, and had a Dutch passport.

Gen. Yitzhak Segev, a very close friend of Gen. Yoffe, was the Israeli military attaché in Iran at that time. Iran was boiling with imminent revolution, but Gen. Segev helped Mike organize a proper truck and bodyguards, coordinating with Dr. Herman Mueller, a German who was serving as the Shah's senior veterinarian. They drove for ten hours, crossing the 4,000 meter high mountains, to reach the Shah's special reserve near the Caspian Sea where the newly-rediscovered fallow deer were located.

In the confusion, Mike managed to get four animals, all females, and drove quickly back to Teheran, as the anti-Shah demonstrations were getting stronger and stronger.

When Mike got to Teheran, thanks to Gen. Segev, he put the four deer in a small enclosure at the Israeli embassy yard until special crates could be fixed and the paperwork completed to get the deer out of Iran.

After a day or two, General Segev received a phone call from Dr. Muller, who was also the authority for export of wild animals, and he said, "Because the revolution is imminent, I am not going to give permission to release your deer unless you agree to take the shah's lion and tiger to safety at the zoo in Germany.

(Gen. Segev purportedly learned from some of his friends in the secret service that Dr. Muller was an ex-Nazi who didn't want to do anything that would help Israel; so Segev knew he couldn't argue with Muller or Muller wouldn't sign the release papers for the animals).

So, even though almost everyone was more concerned with getting PEOPLE out of Iran at the time and we didn't have enough funds to finance this very costly operation with the lion and tiger, we agreed; and, also according to the agreement, some of the offspring would be returned to the Shah's reserve in Iran.

Because mentioning Israel was too dangerous and Dr. Muller was becoming quite difficult, Gen. Segev and Mike tried a new tack, and went to the Dutch ambassador to get documentation that the animals were going to fly to the Amsterdam zoo; so they went to the Dutch ambassador to get his approval.

When it was explained it to him, the Dutch ambassador said: "In the second World War, we succeeded in saving a lot of Jewish people; now I will complete another mission by saving some deer for the Holy Land."

And he signed the papers.

Gen. Segev and Mike still didn't know how to solve the problem of the lion and tiger, but then I think God came into the picture, because that same night there was a very aggressive demonstration; people broke into the Shah's palace grounds, and tore to pieces the lion and tiger which were symbols of the Shah.

The next morning, Dr. Muller was still in shock about the Shah's lion and tiger, and agreed to sign the papers to let the deer travel from Iran to Holland.

So the deer were put on one of the last El Al airplanes that left Iran; and, on the way to Amsterdam with the animals, the plane "landed unexpectedly" at Israel's Ben Gurion airport with

75

the animals, where Gen. Yoffe and some of other nature authority people were waiting—with tears in their eyes.

The deer were ultimately brought to the Hai-Bar Reserve in the Carmel, near Haifa, where their ancestors once lived. They were put in the care of Salach the Druze, who was not a zookeeper or zoologist, but a well-experienced, gentle shepherd that Gen. Yoffe tapped to fulfill this huge responsibility.

You can see more details about the raising and care of the Mesopotamian Fallow deer in the chapter in this book called, "Salach the Druze."

To make a long story short, after about thirty years, Israel has now has the largest herd of Mesopotamian Fallow Deer in the world, with several hundred presently roaming free in the Western Galilee and south of Jerusalem.

The last information we had about the Mesopotamian fallow deer in Iran was from an article written by Iranian and German zoologists in Zoo Yearbook in 1991. They said that Mesopotamian fallow deer in Iran had been heavily hunted; very few survived; and those that did (survive) were in quite poor condition.

Salach, the Druze Shepherd: "Godfather" of the Mesopotamian Fallow Deer in Israel

Salach is an old Druze man with whom I worked for nearly thirty years. I think he should be mounted and put on display as a national treasure of our Country.

He's neither a biologist nor an experienced animal keeper, but "When it comes to animals, Salach knows more than a professor," says Ret. Gen. Yitzhak Segev, who was Israel's military attaché in Iran when the Mesopotamian fallow deer "rescue" took place.

Salach was hand-picked by General Avraham Yoffe—then head of the Nature Reserves Authority—to be the first godfather / teacher / psychiatrist to the precious Mesopotamian Fallow deer which were brought to Israel from Iran at the end of the 70s.

Around 80,000 Druze live in Israel today, most of them in the northern part of Israel. Although their language and food is similar to the Arabs, they don't believe in Muhammad, their religion is secret and different from all other religions, and, among other things, Druze are now an essential part of the Israel army and have reached quite high levels in it.

Gen. Yoffe knew Salach and his family very well because they had constructed all the fences at the Hai-Bar Nature Reserves in Israel. He knew that Salach was an experienced shepherd as well as a very devoted, gentle and wise person, so he asked Salach to take care of the first four precious deer brought from Iran.

Salach, a gentle man, quiet, thoughtful, and pleasant, walks softly and gracefully, and is said to have, "hands of silk."

I believe that Salach's extraordinary treatment and care of these deer was a major reason that Israel went from having no more Mesopotamian fallow deer in the country, to now having the largest herd of Mesopotamian fallow deer in the world!

Thanks to Salach, Godfather of the Mesopotamian fallow deer in Israel, several hundred of these precious creatures are now roaming free in nature in the north, and a few were also released not far from Jerusalem.

Getting the thought-to-be-extinct Persian fallow deer from Iran to Israel was an exciting story, told elsewhere; but, to make a long story short, we were successful in getting four deer out of Iran just before the Shah's reign ended.

Salach recalls that when Gen. Yoffe put the deer in his care, he (Yoffe) said to him: "This is the situation: Either we succeed—or they will disappear completely."

Salach recalls that he said to himself: "I know how big this responsibility is to the whole country—I HAVE TO SUCCEED!"

At that time, we had little or no scientific information about the special, delicate ways to take care of this very rare deer—and Salach was the key to their very successful reintroduction back into Israel.

Soon after we got the four females from Iran, we acquired two additional males from the Baron Von Opel Zoo in Kronstadt, Germany, to round out our breeding nucleus. However, at the quarantine center in Tel Aviv, where all animals are brought and checked before they can be released to other parts of the country, the two German males fought with each other—and one died.

To make the story even more interesting, all the deer that we got from Iran were females; but, most fortunately, three of them were pregnant! That spring, the three pregnant females gave birth at the Hai-Bar Carmel—to three males.

When the first deer was born, Salach says he waited all day so General Yoffe would be the first one to know about it. "I didn't tell even my wife or family or anyone," says Salach—"and when I finally reached General Yoffe, he came rushing to the Hai-Bar—and we both cried together."

Salach mated the female deer with the remaining German male—and the herd took off from there. One of the first male offspring became the dominant male after the old German male died.

But I'm getting ahead of myself.

Salach was so sensitive and concerned about the precious deer and their needs, he often slept close to them. He gave them very special plants to eat that he cut with his sword. He always gave them very clean and fresh water. He helped the devoted vet whenever needed; and his eyes were very sharp to locate sick and wounded animals, as well as which ones to choose to match and mate together.

Another thing Salach did was craft very good shelters that would protect the deer from the most dangerous combination of wind and rain in the winter.

Salach started working with the fallow deer when I was still director of the Haifa Zoo. Because he didn't always have a good supply of quality hay, he came to me one day, told me about the animals, and asked me, in his very rich Hebrew, "Would you close one eye if I 'steal' one bale of hay from you? I promise I will return it some day."

So I closed BOTH my eyes—and gave him two bales!

I was also very interested in these special deer and spent as much time there as I could.

And that was the beginning of a very long friendship, which made me one of the best *labane* (a sour, soft dairy product typical to the Middle East) makers in the Middle East as well as enjoying other rich Druze foods that Salach's family would bring us when they visited him at the Hai-Bar when he was working day and night with the deer.

Not long after that, I was tapped by General Yoffe to become Director of the Wild Animal Protection Sector of Israel's Nature Reserves Authority, and I spent many nights together with Salach taking care of the animals, which I enjoyed so much, and our families became very good friends.

I remember Salach's expertise at moving an animal from one place to another just by knowing them and maneuvering them gently, and using "friendly persuasion."

He would pick the deer we wanted to move, and then he would walk in a certain way, talk to them in a certain way, feed them with concentrated protein pellets that they liked very much, and maneuver them from one place to another without any special gear, restraint or medication. Not to mention that he knew WHICH animal needed to be moved. He could recognize each one, even if they were the same age and size, he always knew who was who.

I also remember the time that Salach went to offer a nice bale of hay to the dominant male in the breeding enclosure, but didn't pay enough attention to the fact that the male was in the middle of his rut (deer mating season), and Salach just happened to walk between the dominant male and one of the rival males who were ready to fight each other for superiority.

A minute later, Salach was in mid-air from a very severe blow from the large antlers of the male, and he crashed to the ground.

The male didn't pay attention to Salach, and turned back to his rival, while Salach managed to crawl out of the enclosure, with a broken hand and wrist.

Salach told me that when he entered the enclosure the next day after this incident, the male "asked him for forgiveness." But since then, even with very good treatment at the local hospital, two of Salach's fingers remained paralyzed.

Two years after that, when Salach was driving home to his Druze village not far from the Hai-Bar Carmel, he swerved to avoid hitting a badger that was crossing the road, and, instead, he crashed into a large rock. He called me to take him to the hospital.

They took care of Salach's broken head; and then, a few days later, his two paralyzed fingers began to work! The hospital specialist said that the strong blow from the accident probably did it in some way.

Salach and Dolly

On the whole subject of acquiring, raising, and growing the herd of fallow deer, Salach says, with typical humility, "Sometimes there's luck as much as brains."

But perhaps Salach's most important contribution was "adopting" an old Dutch couple who used to walk in the Hai-Bar regularly; and, although they spoke English and he couldn't, two cups of very strong Druze coffee made them very good friends.

As the Dutch couple were true animal lovers, they contributed generously to the development of the Carmel Hai-Bar Nature Reserve; and we were able to get a good Jeep, build very good paths, and develop a system of watering the new trees that were planted after a fire.

Perhaps most important, we were able to buy one of the first mobile phones used in our country, which I gave to Salach, and which later saved his life.

One Saturday, I was home resting when I got a call from Salach's new cell phone, but it wasn't Salach on the other end of the line. It was a youngster who told me there had been an accident and to come quickly to the Hai-Bar. I didn't ask too many questions, but I called an ambulance, and I went there as fast as I could.

There I found Salach, nearly unconscious, next to the overturned jeep which had fallen down into the *wadi* (valley), probably due to a brake problem. The young boys had found him under the jeep and called me because the only telephone number that Salach could remember was mine.

81

The ambulance arrived, and, by miracle of the Druze God, combined with the very intensive care Salach received in the hospital, he survived, although he was paralyzed by the accident and now walks with the aid of crutches.

Nobody knows how Salach got out from under the overturned jeep that day, but Salach insists that General Yoffe, who was in heaven then, had lifted the Jeep from his body.

I can't think of a better explanation.

After that, Salach's brother's son, Yakoub, took his place, and is now continuing the tradition with the animals at the Hai-Bar Carmel. Salach's children and relatives were always an essential help when we had to control fires or had other troubles which needed "more hands." And before Yakoub became a helper at the Hai-Bar, he had already helped us many times, as he was a professional fence builder and his physical strength was very useful in carrying things and building fences.

When I wanted to find a way to show gratitude to the younger generation of their family, I paid Salach's and Yakoub's youngest sons a few shekels to catch grasshoppers for our tarantula, which they adored very much—and they showed me how quick and efficient boys could be in catching a jumping cricket.

Most important, I believe the combination of Druze shepherds and fallow deer is an excellent one!

Salach still comes frequently to visit his "children," the fallow deer, at the Hai-Bar Carmel.

And, every year that passes and we both grow older, Salach and I look more and more alike. And, although I can't compete with his large mustache, many people say we are very alike, both in our hearts and in our souls.

I still visit Salach frequently, at his home, where I enjoy the excellent, cool water from his well, the bitter black coffee, and the sweet memories.

Tale of a Caracal's Tail

The caracal is one of the less social wild cats of Israel. It is comparatively large, about the size of a coyote, and has very unique tufts of hair on the top of its ears.

Caracals were once limited to the dry southern part of Israel. They were mostly seen alone, each of them having quite a large territory, about ten square miles or more, and they specialized in eating birds, rodents, reptiles, and sometimes even insects.

When fields for agriculture increased in the northern parts of Israel, leading to increased visits of birds and other animals, the caracals migrated north after them, and now you can find caracals all over the country, up to the Golan Heights. (In the more populated areas of the North, the caracals also began to feed on domestic cats and even small dogs).

Caracals are always active during the night, so it's still not at all common to see caracals in nature.

But before all this took place, something very spectacular happened to me in 1987 when I toured the southern part of the Negev desert with the best Israeli zoologist there ever was, my teacher and friend, Prof. Heinrich Mendelssohn.

Prof. Mendelssohn was what we call in Israel, a "*yekke,*" a very typical "square" German, very naive, and very honest, very pedantic, going into small details. They are also known for their formality. During our desert hike he was wearing a very heavy, thick black coat, even in the hottest place in the desert, while I was wearing shorts and cool shirts.

It was an extremely hot day and I was following clear footprints, which I had identified as caracal footprints.

Although we were exceptionally thirsty and had only a small water supply, the footprints were quite fresh, so I was most anxious to follow them very, very carefully, and not make too much noise so the caracal wouldn't hear us and run away.

After quite a long trek, my intuition told me to look over the top of a small hill. I motioned for Prof. Mendelssohn to join me quietly.

I got down on my stomach and peeked over the top, and there it was...

A mother caracal sat in the shade of a small tree, and she was swinging her tail, and the three cubs near her were jumping, one at a time, to try to catch the tip of the tail.

We were breathless at this sight.

We didn't have a camera, and we didn't want to say a word so they wouldn't run away, so we remained, silently watching for nearly an hour to see how she taught them to hunt.

All the cubs were in good condition, and we also noted from the mother's teats (nipples) that they were still nursing.

We finally and reluctantly retreated, very quietly.

We both knew we had just seen something extraordinary in nature.

We came back with a very deep impression, a very deeply-felt experience (*chavaya*) that we had just shared—and that few, if any, others will ever see.

Sadly, this was one of my last meetings with Prof. Mendelssohn, as he passed away not long after that.

The Fox Who Liked Blue Soup

As part of my army reserves obligation (all Israeli soldiers serve in the reserves after their regular active military service, until about age 50, more or less), I was in charge of a group doing reconnaissance on a high, steep rocky area overlooking Egyptian oil refineries in the Sinai Peninsula, not far from the Suez Canal.

When we arrived, we replaced a well-known paratrooper regiment that had just finished their reserve duty—and they told me there was no electricity, nothing to do there, and very boring,

I was responsible for about fifteen soldiers, some of them not so young, but it was a very interesting group, including soldiers from Morocco, Romania, India, Poland, Russia, Iraq, and, there was even one American.

We were told there "might" be some enemy commando soldiers in the area, so we had to be on guard 24 hours a day.

Apart from this, there was nothing official to do.

Of course, as I like the desert very much, I found, very quickly, many things of interest to me. I found a lot of footprints of insects, rodents, reptiles, and even foxes. I also found a lot of marine fossils as this place probably used to be, millions of years ago, part of an ancient sea.

So, since it was fairly boring for most of the others and there were no other camps near us, I decided to invent something for them to do.

Since the other soldiers were not zoologists, and we had a lot of food products brought by the weekly helicopter, I asked each of the men, a different one each day, to prepare a dinner for us in his national food style.

We were going to be there for nearly a month, so it was very interesting to see how these people would prepare their special food preferences.

Some of their dishes we enjoyed very much; others, like the Indian food, were so spicy we couldn't even touch them.

I told them that, as the commander, I was also part and I had to do it, too.

So one day my turn came.

I was "a complete ignorant" when it came to making food; so I at least remembered that my mother once prepared a chicken soup with all kinds of vegetables.

I told the men that I'd prepare a chicken soup with all kinds of ingredients; and I would put in chicken eggs like my mother used to do. So I prepared the soup using some of the vegetables that we had, including, among others, a purple cabbage.

When the soup was boiling, I added the eggs, and then I think I added what I thought was salt, but it was probably a kind of baking soda and, with the addition of this powder, the soup that looked so nice turned blue!

Except for the color, I thought it was very nice, and I put it in the army plates and I beat on a big pot to call everyone to dinner (except for one guard); I also prepared some salad, and some not-so fresh canned fruit for dessert.

The soldiers came, and they were very happy. They ate the salad, and then I put the soup in their plates, and I saw that they were looking at each other, not saying a word.

I began to eat, but after a few spoonfuls, it seemed like I was the only one eating the soup. It was quite good, but they didn't touch it.

"Try it; it's quite good," I told them.

"Blue is connected with poison," the Romanian answered. "We never eat blue food."

So I think I was the only one to eat the soup; but the salad and the fruit were nice, and it was quite a hot day, so I told them, "We can skip the soup, so don't feel bad, the color is not so appetizing," and the solders all agreed.

To tell you the truth, I was quite offended, because the soup was quite tasty to me, so what could I do? We put all the soup in one big pot, and I took it and threw it over one of the rocks where I had seen a lot of fox footprints, but hadn't yet seen any fox.

Then I waited about 20-30 yards from the rock, behind a dried bush, until it was dark. We had a special army instrument called a "starlight intensifier" that intensified the light of the stars by ten thousand (which was used by the army to identify unwanted enemies in the dark), so I could see quite well, and at about nine or ten o'clock, he came.

The fox didn't like the soup either! But he ate part of the chicken, and I could see that he was not a common fox. He was a Rock fox, (a Blanford's fox), with very tiny paws that enabled him to climb easily on very steep, rocky terrain. He was very very small in comparison to the common fox, and, whenever I moved a little, he would disappear within a second.

The next day, I put a quarter of a container of cottage cheese on the rock. It seemed to me that he preferred it—he had probably never eaten such a thing in his life—so he licked the stone on which I had put the cottage cheese, for a long time.

Every evening after that, I put another few spoonfuls of cottage cheese on the stone, and moved closer to him. I believe he smelled my presence, because at the beginning he would disappear; but as time passed, he let me get closer to him. He would look for quite a long time before beginning to eat, until he saw that there was no movement or threat from me, and he probably couldn't resist his attraction to the cheese.

(I don't know if he told his friends about this, because he always came alone).

The last day before we were scheduled to leave and be replaced by another group of soldiers, I had gotten so close to him that he was about a yard from my hand, taking the cheese from a piece of wood that I held, looking me in the eyes; and I believe he would have said, "thank you," if he could.

It also seemed to me, that during the time of our contact, he gained a few ounces of weight.

So we were picked up from the rock and brought back to Israel.

In my knapsack, I brought back with me a few scorpions I had found quite a distance from where we were camped. These scorpions were not familiar to me, and they were quite different from the species I knew in Israel. And, although I was an expert at catching scorpions, I caught and carried them in small boxes, handling them very carefully, as I was not specifically familiar with them, and didn't want to be strung.

After being examined by Hebrew University experts, these scorpions were described as a "highly deadly," different species than the ones found in Israel. I believe they remain in the university collection to this day.

Rediscovering the Emerald Lizard

"Schnell! Schnell! Schlang! Schlang! (Hurry! Hurry! Snake! Snake!)" screamed excited voices on the other end of my phone.

The garbled cries belonged to several mentally-retarded old men, immigrants from Europe, aged 50 to 60, who worked at a lovely park across from the Hai-Bar Carmel wildlife reserve, keeping it clean and nice.

I thought one of them had been bitten by a snake, but what really happened turned out to be a very fascinating, educational, and satisfying experience for me.

This story begins in 2002, when I was working for the Nature Reserves Authority at the Hai-Bar Carmel near Haifa. That year, I had the good fortune to "rediscover" the beautiful emerald lizard as well as build a new home for the local fire salamander, which is the most southerly location where this species is found.

A few decades earlier, when you would walk through the Nature Park just south of Haifa University (across from the Hai-Bar Carmel Nature Reserve) to enjoy the beautiful Carmel flowers, you would almost always see the most beautiful lizard in Israel—the emerald lizard.

Comparatively large, almost one foot long, and a very vivid bright-green color, the Emerald Lizard is considered by objective people to be the most beautiful in the country. As part of its dazzling beauty, during the mating season, the male Emerald Lizard has a very prominent lower chin speckled with a vibrant turquoise blue.

At any rate, in recent decades, probably because of the increased number of Blue Jays and/or feral, former domestic cats spending a lot of time in the field, we thought we lost this beautiful lizard.

A few well-trained zoologists tried several times to find them in the Carmel and couldn't (although they were still found in the northern part of Israel).

The last time I had personally seen an Emerald lizard was in the mid-90s when I was watching the Griffon vultures in their cage at the Hai-Bar Carmel.

A beautiful male emerald lizard came to catch flies which were landing on the meat which was put out for the vultures. He was so fast, he caught his prey and then quickly disappeared into the dense vegetation of the *wadi*.

A few years later, at the Haifa flea market, I found a beautiful bronze casting of an emerald lizard, which I bought for a relatively large amount of money; and I began to think that I would never again see this beautiful lizard in person.

In fact, I didn't see another one until I got the phone call!

The place where the emerald lizard used to be seen is a very nice park with a lot of ancient remains; it is also is a very popular picnic area with a great scenic view; and this place was being maintained by a few old retarded men as part of a community service that they were able to perform.

To show them my appreciation for their devoted work, I would invite them frequently to the Hai-Bar, give them some light snacks like hummus or *labane* (which they liked very much), and I would tell them about the Carmel animals and plants.

Once, when I was showing them a picture of the footprints of the wild boar and badger, the book was open by chance to a photo of the emerald lizard.

I told them about this beautiful lizard which is quite rare in Israel, and asked them (without any hope, of course), that if they ever saw such a creature, to call me immediately.

After they prepared themselves a very good herbal tea from leaves found in the area, they left—and I forgot about the whole thing.

About two weeks later, I received the excited and strange call on my cell phone, delivered in a garbled mixture of Hebrew and Yiddish.

What I understood from their shouts of "Schlang! Schlang! Schnell! Schnell!" (Snake! Snake! Hurry! Hurry!) was to come quickly to a certain location. As I hurried over, I was quite worried that someone had been bitten by a Palestinian viper, a poisonous snake which is quite common at that location.

When I got there, I was amazed to see a Montpelier snake, a common, large, "semi-poisonous" snake—with one third of the body of an emerald lizard stuffed in his mouth.

I was quite noisy and the snake panicked and dropped the lizard, which was wounded, but still very much alive.

I quickly took the lizard and brought it to the Haifa Zoo where they had good facilities for taking care of reptiles.

A week later I was informed that the emerald lizard was a female, she had begun to eat, and was in quite good physical condition.

Not long after that, a zoology lecturer at Haifa University asked me to assist one of his students to find an interesting subject on which to do research.

I suggested to this student that he make a very thorough search in a few areas for the emerald lizard.

After a week, the student returned to me with about twenty photos he had taken of different emerald lizards in the areas I had recommended.

I couldn't believe it, so I offered to go with him the following week to see it with my own eyes.

It turned out that this student had the unique ability to hear the lizards rustling in the leaves or bushes.

We were walking along, when suddenly he stopped me and said, "Do you hear a noise in the dense pistachio shrubs about five meters from us?" Since my hearing is not too good, I said, "No, I can't hear it."

So we approached the shrub very carefully. He moved one of the branches of the shrub to the side—and there it was—a beautiful emerald lizard!

A few minutes later, under a mound of dry leaves, he heard another lizard walking, and we found it.

That day, we "only" found six emerald lizards!

I still feel that this whole sequence of events regarding the emerald lizard was pure luck.

It just goes to show that an old zoologist can learn a lot from elderly retarded men who found the first one—and a young student with excellent hearing, who found many!

The Treasure Cave

The following story isn't really about animals. Nevertheless it is something that made a big impression on me that lasts to this day—and the story does have a few centipedes and spiders in it!

I was probably about 11 or 12 years old when something strange and wonderful—something every child dreams of—happened to me.

Although I had visited a certain deserted field near my home many times to collect scorpions and vipers for the zoo director in Jerusalem, I never realized the field concealed other amazing treasures.

One day I tried to move an extremely heavy rock to see if I might find a scorpion or a snake under it. I couldn't move the rock, so I used a long iron bar to pry underneath it. After quite some time and a lot of sweat, I finally pushed the rock to the side.

Under the rock was a big, dark hole.

I couldn't see anything in the dark hole, so I widened it with the iron bar. It took about an hour of digging until I was able to crawl inside and see that it went off to the right. The space got wider after a meter, but it was very dark. I couldn't see anything, and, to tell you the truth, I was a little afraid.

So, after putting a lot of thorns and dry plants over the hole to camouflage it, I went home. When I returned to the concealed hole the next day, I brought a few candles and matches with me.

It took me half an hour to crawl through a very narrow, humid, and stale-smelling passage, and when I succeeded in lighting the candle, I saw that I was inside a big cave, very dark, full of cobwebs, with a few empty containers and old empty cans lying on the ground along with old newspapers written in Arabic.

I also remember when I entered that there were many centipedes and a box of old keys. I took a few of the keys home with me and since then I have learned they were used for winding old clocks.

In the corner of the cave, covered with a lot of dust, were about 25 very old rifles, many of them with mother-of-pearl inlaid decorations. And when I held one, although it was a little rusted, I could still smell the oil that had been used to clean and preserve it. Even though I didn't know it at the time, guns of that age and decoration were quite rare.

At that moment I believed I was the luckiest child in the world. Although there was no gold, no silver, no precious stones, for me it was truly a treasure! I was afraid to take the guns home because they were big and I didn't know where to hide them. Every few days, I enjoyed crawling into my secret cave and playing with the guns, most of which were only capable of firing black powder.

So I kept this secret inside me for a couple of weeks—not even telling my parents who always seemed too busy to talk to me anyway. After three weeks or a little more, I was bursting with my secret and felt that I had to tell someone else about it, maybe to boast. So I confided in a neighbor boy. After making him swear not to tell anyone, I took him to my treasure cave.

Not long afterwards, I had to go to another town for vacation with my parents.

When I came back I hurried to my cave, but when I got there all the guns were gone! I didn't have any proof, but my theory was that my "friend" had probably told somebody, like his father, or somebody else, and they came and took my guns away.

If I owned those old rifles today, I'd be a very rich man. Even so, I still remember how rich I felt when I played with the rifles and the joy of discovering of my own secret treasure cave.

Losing the guns taught me a good lesson: It's important to choose your friends carefully—also to choose carefully what you tell them and do with them!

Reptiles Have Lives, Too

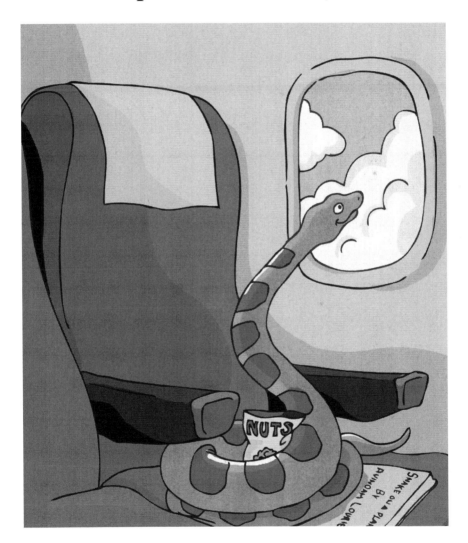

Snakes on a Bus & Snakes on a Plane

In 1973, I visited the United States to see my friend and colleague, the late Sneed Collard II, who was then a Professor of Zoology at the University of West Florida in Pensacola.

Of course I wanted to see and do as much as I could when I was in the US, so I bought a $99 ticket on the Greyhound Bus and traveled to Los Angeles, where I had a place to stay. From there, I went to the San Diego Zoo, which I considered to be the "Mecca of Zoos."

At the San Diego Zoo, I met the local herpetologist who was quite interested in getting some Middle East species of snakes for their collection.

I told him that I would do my best to send him some nice Middle East snakes. As gratitude, he gave me a very nice milk snake and a very nicely-colored corn snake, both quite harmless.

A few miles before Los Angeles, our bus from San Diego was stopped—and two border patrol policemen boarded it. (I think they were looking for drugs).

There were several Mexicans on the bus—and, having just fought in the Yom Kippur War, my skin was dark from the sun. I also had a nice, big black mustache, so they may have thought I was Mexican.

"Get off of the bus, and take all your belongings into the station," they commanded. When it was my turn to be checked, they asked for my passport, which I had left where I was staying in Los Angeles, so their suspicion increased as to what I had in the two plastic boxes.

I didn't want to tell them that I had snakes, so I told them, "I have some biological materials."

They looked up and said, with a certain grin (meaning they didn't believe me), "Let us see 'the biological materials.'" (They had already found marijuana in one of the parcels belonging to one of the Mexicans on the bus).

It was quite hot in the station in the middle of summer, so when I opened the first box, the corn snake just sprang out quickly.

I couldn't believe what happened next: The big border patrol guys were so shocked, they ran, like the fastest sprinters there ever were, and they "attached" themselves to the far wall, so to speak.

After they left the room, a voice, from a loudspeaker, like the voice of God from above, asked me, "Did you put the monsters back into the box?"

"Yes," I said.

"We have held another bus for you," the voice said. "Go away. Get on. Go."

And so I did. (And I still marvel at the way a small, innocent snake overwhelmed a couple of big policemen).

Snakes on a plane...

When it came time to go home from the same trip that had included stops in Florida, California, and New York, I prepared to head back to Israel with the snakes, two lizards, and one tarantula in my bag.

In order not to cause suspicion, I put the creatures into empty cigar boxes, given to me by my cousin who was the Israeli consul in New York at that time.

There weren't any security checks yet in those days, but after I was on the airplane for a few hours, I wanted to check and see if there was enough air in the boxes.

Everyone on the plane was asleep, so, very carefully and quietly, I opened each box, and found that all the creatures were there—except one of the snakes.

I looked through all the other parts of my bag—and couldn't find the snake.

I looked under the carpet.

Just then, the flight attendant came by and asked: "What are you doing in the middle of the night?"

"I dropped two dollars worth of coins," I lied.

After she left, I searched a bit more, but I never found the snake.

So, if he didn't die, he's probably still there!

Snake Mistakes
Education of Wife: The Wrong Approach

Somewhere along the way, I wanted to find a way to lower my wife's fear of snakes—and since I thought that I was such a good psychologist, I could convince her to touch, and even like snakes.

But now I have to admit that my wife probably got her fear of snakes "from the milk of her mother" and there's not much I could do about it.

Since my wife liked old, nice vases, I brought home a very nice vase with a very innocent and quiet, small snake in it, with a very nice cotton net over the top of the vase to prevent the snake from getting out.

I showed her the innocent, quiet snake, and told her that this was "a new Japanese toy," very complicated, with a lot of springs that would move with any slight air movement—and I took out the snake and showed her that it felt and acted like a real snake.

She touched it and said, "Unbelievable, it feels very real."

So I put it back in the vase and went to get something to eat.

While I was gone, she got closer to the vase to look at the snake more closely, and, since all the windows were closed and there was no breeze, she realized that the snake was moving by itself. She thus concluded, correctly, that the snake's movements were not caused by the wind!

When I came back into the room, the look I got from her showed me—that I had just lost again!

Poisonous Snakes on My Doorstep

When I was director of the Wildlife Conservation Department of Israel's Nature Reserves Authority in the mid-80s, there was a wave of German herpetologists coming to Israel to catch poisonous snakes for their collections.

I still don't know what they found in our poisonous snakes, especially desert poisonous snakes, but we did a lot of surveillance, especially at the airport, to stop them from taking out snakes that were considered to be "protected animals."

What we didn't know is that some of them had contacted a local, amateur herpetologist, and, after several very thorough interrogations of local herpetologists, we discovered that, on a certain date, a certain woman, the girlfriend of an Israeli herpetologist, was going to put about 30 poisonous snakes in small cotton bags into her handbag, and try to smuggle them out of the country.

We succeeded in getting the flight number, and our people waited at the airport—and got the snakes—but, as it was a Friday and it would be the Jewish Sabbath, I had to keep the snakes over the weekend before I could send them back to the desert where they belonged. So I planned to keep them at home.

I took all the bags of snakes, and when I got home, I discovered that I didn't have the key to the front door, so I left the bag at the door, went to the nature reserve, and after an hour and a half, I came back home, where I found the following note on the entrance to my house:

"You are crazy, I am going to leave you forever."

It was signed by my wife.

The neighbor called me over and told me that when my wife came back from work, carrying one of our kids in her arms, she started up the stairs, and ran into five poisonous desert snakes that were going down the stairs!

She succeeded to reverse quickly, and then, of course, went to her sister's house to cry.

Then I realized what had happened: I had left the bag in an area that was shady and cool, but by the time I came back, the sun had moved and heated the bag—and some of the snakes—actually, about eight of them—had succeeded in getting out—and they were probably now in my yard!

It took me quite a long time, but I found six of them (which meant two of them were still missing)!

I would have been more worried, but since the snakes were from the south, I didn't think they could survive our northern winter in Haifa, and they probably eventually died.

A Disappointing Reptile Exhibition...

Another of my first, self-determined missions as director at the Haifa Zoo was to combat the fear and disgust that some people had of reptiles. Since there was no known reptile exhibition in Israel at the time, I thought this would be an original project to attract more people to come to visit our comparatively small zoo.

So, with some local volunteers, including children who were very interested in reptiles, plus some older people with a lot of motivation to help (and knowledge of how to build a terrarium for a reptile exhibition), we prepared and opened, within the second year, the first reptile exhibit in Israel.

The exhibition contained not only local reptiles, but also many poisonous and non-poisonous snakes from all over the world (of course we had anti-venoms on hand in case of accidents).

The public was very enthusiastic about the reptile exhibition, we got a lot of positive publicity, and thousands of people came. I invited the elected politicians of the Haifa Municipality to come and visit the zoo so they could see and appreciate how their money was being used. After showing them around the zoo in general, I took them to the new reptile exhibition where they spent more than an hour, without even asking one question.

After the show, I asked the Vice Mayor how he liked it, and, to my complete shock and dismay, he replied, "It's the most disgusting thing that I've ever seen."

I was extremely disappointed, I guess because I expected politicians to have more empathy for poisonous reptiles than that.

Scorpions Get Knocked Down on Shabbat

When I was about 12, one of my first paying jobs was to sell poisonous yellow scorpions to an elderly zoology professor who was then director of the old Biblical Zoo in Jerusalem. He used them to produce the first anti-venom against yellow scorpion bites.

And it was a way that I could earn a few dollars.

To deliver the scorpions, I would ride my bike, carrying a big wooden box of scorpions under my arm, or sometimes a live Palestinian viper in one hand while I steered my bike with the other.

But when I delivered scorpions on a Saturday, I had to pass through the very religious quarter of Jerusalem, and they didn't want cars or bikes or anything passing through their area on the Sabbath!

Although I would ride through the area early in the morning, there was often someone waiting in ambush to show their displeasure by throwing stones and bottles at me.

I usually avoided them, but once, one of their missiles thrown from a window hit my shoulder and I fell from my bike, dropping my box of scorpions on the road.

The scorpions scattered.

I was able to recover all but two of them. I knew how many I had because I got paid half a *grush* (about a penny) for each scorpion I delivered.

So, in addition to the blow to my shoulder, I lost a bit of my "salary" that day.

A Reptile Show with a Twist

One day, when I was in my office in Jerusalem (as part of the Wild Animal Protection Section of the NRA), there was a knock at the door.

A young man wearing a long, black frock coat and black hat, as well as having two curly sidelocks of hair (*payot*) that the most religious Jews have, entered, and said to me: "I live in *Mea Shaarim* (the religious sector of Jerusalem). I would like to expand the horizons of the people there by showing them a nice display of snakes and lizards of the world; and I need from you a permit to do this."

"Ok, very nice," I said to him. "I can tell that you're very interested, but you have to know how to keep them, what to feed them, what kind of temperatures to maintain, etc."

"Where can I learn?" he interrupted.

"Books," I answered, "but I suggest you go to Tel Aviv University and meet an experienced zoologist, Professor Heinrich Mendelssohn, who is a well-known professor there. I will speak to him, and I will give you some books; and you can work with him and learn about the reptiles at the Tel Aviv collection."

"After you spend a few months there, come back to me," I said; "and, if you know what you're talking about, I will give you the permit—as long as you have a place to make this 'serpentarium'."

"I have a place," he said, and then he left.

I forgot all about it; but a few weeks later, I received a call from Prof. Mendelssohn.

Before I could speak, Prof. Mendelssohn said, "What did you do to me? Believe it or not, the kid is a genius. I gave him a few books about reptiles and he came to me and knew most of the books by heart. I tested him," Prof. Mendelssohn went on. "He knew the scientific names. He knew the ecology, etc."

"He was a very good worker at our reptile display," Prof. Mendelssohn continued, "and I think he is really ready to keep the snakes—he knows the dimensions of the displays, how to take care of them, and what to do."

"So, you know what?" Prof. Mendelssohn concluded. "I'm sending him back. He has been sleeping near one of the cages in a sleeping bag. He doesn't have money for a hotel. He is reading the religious books. He is not missing even one prayer—and he is one of a kind," said Prof. Mendelssohn.

A few days later, the young man came to me and said, "Did he tell you that I'm much more advanced now? Ask me a few questions."

And I did, and he knew more than a student studying for a B.Sc. degree.

The young man invited me to come and see the place he had chosen for his reptile exhibit in *Mea Shaarim*.

When I got there, I saw a big hall, the size of a wedding hall, and, without asking me, he had already bought special terrariums for reptiles and furnished them with heating apparatus, lights, and everything. He also already had stands for the terrariums built by a carpenter.

He told me that as soon as I would give him the permit, he was ready to get the reptiles from dealers in the United States.

"What about food? Electricity? Cleaning? Safety?" I asked.

"We are going to ask a very cheap entrance fee," he said "and, believe it or not, we will get many people, because in old biblical language, the wild animals are called *M'niflaot ha-boreh*, 'God's wonders', which means something special to religious people."

"And one more thing you have to know," he went on, "is that men and women can't come at the same time. We will have special days for men and special days for women. That's the law. I can't do it otherwise," he said.

There was a lot of publicity about the reptile show in the papers, including photographs; and, a few weeks later, the young man went to the airport to get the reptiles which he had ordered from professional dealers.

He brought about sixty reptiles to the place—lizards; snakes from America, Africa and Asia (most of which were quite common and quite easy to keep); two Israeli Palestinian vipers; a black rat snake; a chameleon; a very colorful milk snake; king snakes from the US; and also some monitors (big lizards); snapping turtles; and more.

He even had a special room where he kept mice and rats and small invertebrates to feed the reptiles.

The first month, the exhibit was open nearly twenty hours a day because there were such a huge number of people who were interested in seeing it. After a month, the exhibit was still extremely popular and he had gotten a nice sum of money from entry fees.

I checked the place twice. It was clean and nice, with youths supervising the visitors not to tap on the glass or to frighten the animals.

This went on for about two months.

And then the whole thing collapsed.

He disappeared.

Some of the reptiles were not alive when we found them. The remainders were sent to Tel Aviv University.

I didn't know why he disappeared.

And the whole story ended quite abruptly and cruelly.

I ran into him nearly a year later. I didn't recognize him. He had short hair; earrings in his ears; no hat—and he didn't look religious at all!

To tell the truth, I was amazed.

"What happened?" I asked. "Why didn't you tell me about this? How could you do such a thing?"

And then he told me the story: "I don't know how to tell you," he said. "I discovered after some time that I am a homosexual, and, unexpectedly, my religious friends discovered it too, and they wanted to kill me because this is against the religion."

He told me that he had to run away quickly to save his life; and, to change his appearance, he threw away the religious clothes and switched to open-collared shirt, pants, and sandals, and had gone to live as a homosexual in Tel Aviv.

As he was quite knowledgeable about animals and didn't know what else to do to make a living, he worked in a pet shop.

"Believe it or not, I was quite successful," he said. "I flew abroad to South America where I lived freely as a homosexual. And now I am back here, although I have no connection with my family or with my old acquaintances."

"I am now living in Tel Aviv," he said, "and my next trip will be to buy a small pet shop in a Haifa Mall."

And that's what he did.

Fake Snake Puts Baboons
"Off Their Feed"

A short time after I began working as Director of the Haifa Zoo, I was asked by our librarian to help her elder son with a small biology project as part of his obligations for his secondary school.

After some thought, I remembered something I had seen a few days earlier, when, in one of the Guenon monkey cages, there were many shouts and hysterics because a poisonous snake (a Palestinian viper which came from a wild *wadi* near the zoo) had entered their cage to drink some water.

So I told the young guy who needed a project, "Let's check and see if the old baboons, which have been in captivity for several generations and have never met snakes, as far as we know, would react to a snake in their cage."

We bought a very good, very realistic-looking plastic snake, and put it on the top of the baboons' food delicacies the next day. There was some activity by the baboons, but they didn't dare to get close to the food the whole day.

The student was watching them the whole time and reported that, even during the night, the baboons went to sleep without eating anything.

Next morning, I suggested putting a branch inside the cage to see if the baboons would use it. It took around two hours until one of the oldest females, but not a dominant female, took the branch, approached the plastic snake, and, with the branch, pushed the snake to the side of the cage, far away from the food.

Then she took the nicest apple. But before she could taste it, the dominant male approached quickly, hit her, and must have said in baboon language: "Well, you are wiser, but I am the dominant male, so I get to eat first!!!"

And, of course, as a dominant male myself, I understand this behavior.

The Mongoose & the Viper

Here's an interesting story I was told by an old zoology professor (Prof. Shulov) who was director of the Biblical Zoo where I would supply vipers and scorpions for the production of anti-venom.

"Many years ago we were not sure how mongooses got to be so efficient at killing poisonous snakes like the Palestinian viper.

Thus the following argument ensued: "Who teaches the mongoose the technique to kill the viper? Is it the mother or is it instinctive?"

"So," he told me, "once we had a very young mongoose with its eyes still closed and nearly naked; and we fed him with a special kind of milk, and when he opened his eyes, the first animals he saw were us."

"And thus this mongoose became a very good friend to all the laboratory crew."

They fed him delicacies. He would play with them; he liked to sit on the shoulder of the old professor and play with his ear. And the mongoose was quite delightful. He was very clean and did all his digestive functions in a small box with gravel and sand.

He also ate a large variety of foods, including milk. But he had never been exposed to snakes.

So, after more than a year, the professor decided that it was the time to get the answer: Would this mongoose be able to kill a snake although he had never learned it from anyone?

The mongoose was kept in a huge container with very smooth walls, so he couldn't get away. Sometimes he was fed there, so he was familiar with the surroundings. Into the middle of this container, the professor put a poisonous, two-foot-long Palestinian viper.

Right away, the mongoose was not happy about this. He was shivering and dancing around; his hair stood on end; he had many signs of agitation, but he didn't get close to the snake for about forty minutes, and then, some, probably hidden, voice told him, "do it."

And the mongoose began to get closer to the snake; and whenever he got too close, the snake tried to bite him; but the mongoose quickly retreated, and the snake couldn't touch him.

After more than half an hour of confrontation, the mongoose became quite tired; but as a last resort, he succeeded in jumping on the snake's head, grabbed him by the back of the head, and killed him.

And, although he was quite hungry, it took him quite some time before he ate the snake.

The second time we did this experiment, he finished the snake in about 25 minutes.

We tried it several times later, and it was never less than 20 minutes.

The timing in nature is much faster.

So what was the answer? Instinct or mother's teaching?

The professor told me, "I'm not sure, but I think he gets the instinct in his blood, and the mother improves the technique."

But then one of the elder workers of the laboratory asked the professor a more important question:

"How could you expose our dearest mongoose without a tear?"

The professor smiled and said, "I forgot to tell you that, without you knowing, a few days earlier, I took the two poison glands out of the snake, so he was not poisonous."

This should probably teach you, don't trust old professors.

Animals Know No Borders

Roe Deer from Tuscany a la Fellini!

In the mid 1990s when I was working as Director of the Hai-Bar Nature Reserve in the Carmel near Haifa, we initiated procedures to reintroduce roe deer back to Israel. (Roe deer went extinct from Israel around 1912).

And, according to the IUCN, The International Union for the Conservation of Nature and Natural Resources (the world's main authority on the conservation status of species), "The last species to disappear should be the first to be reintroduced."

They do it this way because it is assumed that ecological changes are comparatively minor in such a short period of time.

We checked several places from which to get roe deer. We couldn't find a source in the Middle East because of "not ideal" relations with our neighbors. And, since Israel is the most southern location where roe deer have lived, they are very common in Europe; so we tried several sources in Europe.

First, we brought a group of roe deer from Holland, but most of them died immediately upon arrival at the Hai-Bar Carmel because there was a hailstorm on the way from the airport to the Hai-Bar, the truck was open, and the noise of the hail on the crates caused the deer to die from shock.

Another group we got a few months later died during a very severe arson fire at the Hai-Bar Carmel.

Next, we were given a group of roe deer as a present from an organization of hunters in Hungary, but to our sorrow, they were full of very dangerous parasites.

Then I was involved with bringing about ten roe deer from a nature reserve in France; but we didn't breed them well and only a few survived.

So, after a lot of thinking and advice from other sources, I initiated a meeting with a group in Tuscany, Italy.

Tuscany, while not totally similar, was quite close to our ecological conditions in terms of plants, climate, etc.—and we already had a few friends in Tuscany.

So I traveled to the small village of Semproniano, Italy. With just a few hundred inhabitants, Semproniano was a beautiful location, boasting varied ecological habitat, good weather, and good people.

First, I met with the local veterinarian who was in charge of a small, fenced nature area where they put many orphaned roe deer which had been brought to them by local farmers.

One of my strongest memories was of my first Italian lunch with my hosts, at a quaint local restaurant. Lunch consisted of excellent pasta called gnocchi, a good local red wine; and the climax was the Gorgonzola, a typical Italian blue cheese with which I instantly fell in love.

A short distance from the restaurant stood the only hotel of this small village, with only about eight rooms. The owner was an attractive widow who showed me my large, simple, plain room with not too many decorations, save a big cross on the wall with Jesus on it.

Then came the work at the nature area.

Some of the deer were injured and some of them were sick when they were brought to the nature area, but the sanctuary saved most of them by giving them goat's milk and special veterinary care.

Some of the deer were shy, and others were not afraid of those who took care of them. The area where the Roe deer were kept was several hectares in size (one hectare = 2.47 acres).

The nature group had agreed to donate some of these Roe deer to our Hai-Bar Nature Reserve as part of a good relationship with the Holy Land, so we began to make preparations for catching some of the deer and shipping them to Israel.

First, we went to the local carpenter in the village to prepare proper crates so the deer could breathe, couldn't move around too much risking breaking a leg or damage their body; and so they could lie down on some edible hay during the trip.

Then we had to catch the deer in order to take blood samples for bacteriological and parasitological purposes before we could take any with us.

We also had to arrange that the airplane in which they would fly to Israel (in the baggage compartment) would be ventilated, and also heated a little, so the deer wouldn't freeze.

I was there about ten days for this project. Most evenings I spent with my hosts, "learning to be more resistant to the Italian alcohol," enjoy the fine spaghetti, excellent olive oil, and local fruits. I also enjoyed long talks with Sophia, the hotel director, about her life in this small village, and her hopes and dreams. I learned many Italian words, and I also told her about life in Israel.

Catching the roe deer

After we bought the airplane tickets for the deer and prepared the crates, the time arrived to catch the roe deer. We had long, flexible plastic nets into which to drive the deer and then catch them, but the main problem was that we needed several people to help us.

So, with the help of the local vet, we enlisted the local butcher, the local bank clerk, the local pub owner, the local chef, the local undertaker, and the... well, you get the idea!

I was "the conductor, the maestro."

I stood on a big fuel barrel, and with hand signals of a symphony conductor (conducting a very exciting opera, of course)—and with the aid of a translator, I directed the "helpers" where to go, what to do, and when to make noise and herd the deer in a particular direction.

We had to guide the animals into the standing nets—you have to do it in a very sophisticated way so that when they reach the net, you grab them up and put them into a crate—being careful of their sharp antlers.

While we were doing this, the sky opened and rain began to fall. But what a rain! A very heavy rain. And, as I stood there, completely wet, with all the nice people who were helping, I noticed that some of them took bottles of *grappa* (fermented grape drink) from their pants pockets to "help them feel better," because it was very cold out in the rain that day.

It seemed to me that only Fellini was missing from this picture of roe deer scattering every which way, strange guy from Israel conducting, undertaker, butcher and pub owner running around, heavy rain, bottles of Grappa, etc.

We succeeded in catching four females and four males in a few hours, without even one of them (or us) breaking his neck or his leg—even though the "helpers" were very close to physical breakdown themselves! They were so wet—and some of them were even bleeding from this work.

After covering each deer's head with a special cloth to keep them calm, we took a blood sample from each.

When we were done, we all went together to the pub, sang many Italian songs, got drunk, slept for a few hours, probably on the ground—and, in the early light, we checked the crates—and found all of the deer in better condition than we were!

After a day, we got the lab checks back, and they were perfect.

When we got the deer to the Hai-Bar Carmel in Israel, we transferred them to several fenced enclosures with a variety of good, edible Carmel vegetation, and with good places to hide. We also gave them special food pellets and water—plus a lot of love from the Druze Ranger and me.

In each enclosure we put one male and one female, hoping they would settle down together.

Not many months passed, and in two of the enclosures the first "*sabra*" deer were born, two "bambis" in each enclosure.

118

In the following years, all pairs had young, and we planned the first release on a distant hill at the southern Carmel Mountain, where the number of jackals was low, there was a permanent water source, and many tasty plants.

These special deer from Tuscany were the source of all the roe deer in Israel today which were successfully released, and now live FREE and happy in the southern part of the Carmel.

I estimate that there are now about fifty roe deer in Israel. They are very shy and are active at night and in the early morning.

It's not so easy to follow their survival in nature because most of the transmitters that we put on the released deer are no longer functional due to the limited life of the batteries.

But we do see new, young roe deer without any collars, which means they were born in nature. However, since we can't follow them by the transmitter activity any more; and, as they are very shy animals and the vegetation is quite dense, we can't see them, so we don't really know how many were born.

And since there is not enough funding for follow up, we count on periodic observations that are just a matter of chance.

Afterthought: I feel that, as an old zoologist now, I am closing a circle—to breed and release roe deer back to Israel—where the first zoologist killed the last one about a hundred years ago.

Saving a Baby Elephant (& Myself) In Liberia

In the late 80s, I was asked by the US-based Friends of Animals Organization to help build and develop a new system of nature and wildlife preservation in Monrovia, Liberia.

In Liberia at that time nature appreciation was not yet really developed. To give you an idea, I was told that just before I got there that they had discovered a new species of mongoose that had never been seen before. Other interesting animals of that country included a species of dwarf hippopotamus and a large variety of monkeys, including chimpanzees; many bird species; and especially many colorful insects.

So I went to the United States in order to meet and travel to Liberia with a naturalist and zoologist named Bill Clark who was part of the American organization.

Unfortunately, Liberia was on the edge of revolution when we got there. I was in touch with both the US and Israeli embassies in Monrovia, and they told me there was some trouble.

In fact, there was a lot of tension in Liberia because of the war—and a lot of hunger. Fighting broke out while we were there, rebels pushed the regulars back to the capital city of Monrovia, and the government of General Doe began to fail because opposition General Taylor got a lot of help from Sierra Leone.

Nevertheless, when we arrived at Monrovia, we were taken to the large quarantine-fenced center to which animals would be brought.

Our job was to build proper facilities and train the local people how to acquire and take care of the animals, especially monkeys, which, sad to say, were kept by people as entertainment—or food.

One of the ironies I noticed was that there was a lot of singing and happiness among the people, as well as a lot of desperation—a very mixed atmosphere.

And a lot of hunger.

I saw that they cooked monkeys in big pots and sold them along the main travel routes as food.

We hadn't had many days to acclimatize when we got a telephone call from a Dutch tourist, phoning us from a small, distant village.

"Local hunters shot and killed a big female elephant," he said, excitedly. "I've been trying to care for her baby," he continued, "but the baby has a big wound on its hind leg and a lot of health problems and I don't know what to do," he said.

After a few minutes of talking to him, we understood that he had given the baby elephant some cow's milk; however, the elephant was quite sensitive to the fat in the milk, and it caused very severe diarrhea.

As he described the baby elephant and the mother, we speculated that these elephants lived in the forest, and were likely a type of elephants that are a little different—and rarer than the common elephant—which justified our decision to get an airplane and go to save this one elephant!

And, seeing as the Dutchman probably couldn't get proper milk for the elephant, plus the fact that the elephant was injured and quite rare, Bill and I decided to go and bring the baby elephant back to Monrovia as fast as possible—even though the village was quite a distance away.

How could we get there?

Cars were not the answer because there were many rebels along the route.

We decided we had to fly.

121

After some checking, we found an army general whom we invited to a good restaurant. After he was full of food and drink and quite enjoying the jokes of Bill Clark, he said he was willing to help us get an army airplane for our trip.

Although he said it "wasn't a new airplane," he lowered the price from the thousands of dollars that he wanted at the beginning, down to a few hundred—thanks to the nice dinner—and my experience in "Middle East bargaining."

He arranged for us an old airplane for the cost of a few hundred dollars—an old DeHavilland, from World War I.

And then we found a middle-aged, "not-too-sober" English pilot who knew the airplane; and, for the price of a good bottle of Chivas Regal, he was very agreeable, and we didn't have to bargain at all for what we paid him.

This man seemed to be in his late forties, very skinny, not bald, and not very stable when he walked, probably because of the alcohol; and it was difficult to understand his English because he had a kind of Cockney accent.

When we got to the airport to look at the airplane, the pilot turned on the engine and a large cloud of black smoke came out. We were afraid to fly in this airplane, but the pilot said it was "more or less ok" to do so.

So the next day, Bill and I and the pilot took off. I remember that we were very cold when we were in the air because the rear part of the airplane wasn't closed tightly.

After about an hour and a half of flying, we got to the village where the elephant was located.

When I looked down, I saw a huge green "carpet", and a very small brown patch, and the pilot said the small brown patch was the landing spot.

"How can you land on such a thing," I asked.

"I call it a 'bump landing'," he answered.

Bump he did, and when the airplane came to a stop, about ten Black people, half naked, came to the plane carrying a cage made of branches.

Inside the cage was the baby elephant, which was about the size of a small horse (about 3.2 feet long and about 3 feet high). They put the cage with the elephant into the back of the airplane.

Then, without our ok, about seven wounded soldiers, part of the Liberian president's forces, got on the plane—many of them with bandages, all of them with their weapons ready to shoot, some of them seemed to be quite ill, with high fevers.

As the engine started and the airplane began to move, the poor baby elephant had a diarrhea attack, spraying his waste product all over everybody on the plane.

The soldiers, who were already very nervous, became upset about the elephant's diarrhea and the bad smell—and they began to fiddle with their guns. We were afraid that one of them would pull the trigger without intending to do so.

When we were in the air, the baby elephant began to cry. We tried giving him several things, but he refused. The only thing that worked was for me to put my hand in his mouth and let him suck it, which I did, and then he became relaxed.

The problem for me was that I had to stand up in the airplane for two hours with my arm bent at an uncomfortable angle, reaching into the baby elephant's mouth, like a human pacifier!

After one hour of flight, the pilot called us urgently, pointing down to show us that some unidentified people were shooting at us, and then he said, "Hold on tight; I'm going to climb above the clouds."

When I looked at the airplane wings, I could see that there were already a few bullet holes in them.

After a very long time (for us), we landed at the Monrovia airport, and we were welcomed by nice music, played by locals. A high officer met us and told us that President Doe had decided he wanted the elephant for his private zoo.

After very quick thinking, we told him that the elephant was very sick and might transmit very dangerous diseases to them that should be taken care of before he could be placed in the president's collection (which wasn't true—but I asked the general if he wanted to smell the elephant to support what I told

123

him—but finally they let us go and told us that they would take the elephant in a week).

When we got to our base, good milk and a large amount of soft hay was ready for the baby elephant; a proper mixture with coconut oil was also ready; and we were all together on the hay giving him food and calming him down.

I was completely exhausted and very eager to get to my own modest hotel room for an essential shower and some rest. But the moment we left the elephant, he began to cry again, like a baby. I couldn't leave—and so I stayed there. He was lying near me with his trunk on my chest, and we both fell into a very deep sleep until morning. (How can I explain how it felt when the elephant put his trunk around my body because he needed and trusted me? I felt tired, stinky, and wonderful, and as if I had gone to heaven).

In the morning, we were replaced by others to take care of him.

Following very intensive treatment of the wound on the elephant's rear leg, and a few days of rest, the diarrhea stopped, and he began to gain weight and get better, and also formed a very good relationship with one of the older women who was helping us.

After a few more days, the rebels got very close to Monrovia, and all the tourists and other foreign nationals were told to get out of the country. We were very late in being notified, and, with the help of the American embassy, we left the country on the last airplane out, in the first class section, at the very last minute. (This was my first, and probably my last, time to fly in first class).

I think Bill and I were the last White men to leave Monrovia, and even on the way to the airplane, we were stopped by people with uniforms—and we bought our lives by giving them each five dollars!

A few months after I returned to my work at the Hai-Bar Carmel near Haifa, we had a VIP visitor, the American Ambassador.

I gave him a very nice guided tour of the Hai-Bar Reserve; and, at the end I asked him to check on the elephant in Monrovia, where rebels had killed General Doe and taken over.

A few months passed, and one day the ambassador called my house and told me about the young elephant we had saved.

My heart just sank when the ambassador told me he learned from his intelligence, that a few months earlier, the baby elephant had been eaten by hungry people.

Helping Build a Zoo in the West Bank

On a typical day in the mid-80's, at 6 a.m., my phone rang.

I answered, and immediately recognized the voice on the other end as Uri Baidets, General Director of Israel's Nature Reserves Authority, where I worked at the time.

Without apologizing for the early hour, he said, "Do you want to do something interesting?"

Without waiting for my reply, he continued, "Late last night I received a telephone call from the very close inner circle of Prime Minister (Yitzhak) Rabin. He wants us to show the people of the West Bank that we are also human and humane; we want to give them and their children something that will make them very happy."

"We want you to meet with the Mayor of the town of Kalkilya and help him build a modest zoo," Uri continued, "The Mayor of Kalkilya has the land and Israel is funding this." (Kalkilya is located close to the border in the central West Bank, about 30 km northeast of Tel Aviv as the crow flies—and not far from Kfar Saba, which is a small city on the Israel side).

As I recall, the (political) climate at that time, the early-to-mid 80s, was not so positive for Israel, and this would be a very nice positive way to show them a different face of us.

So I went to meet the Mayor of Kalkilya.

I crossed the border with a special pass and went directly to Kalkilya's municipal building.

When I entered the building, I was checked by a few guards wearing very heavy coats (even though it was summer). Under their coats, I noticed that they had automatic submachine guns and some grenades—and who knows what else? I even caught a glimpse of a Tommy gun.

When I entered the Mayor's visiting room, there was a good herbal tea and some sweets. The Mayor said to me, "Drink the tea." And then he began to speak:

"I just want you to know that our people, although many of them are hunters, really like animals," he said, "and, as there are not enough places for the young generation to enjoy, I intend to build a zoo, and also a restaurant, and a big pool with small boats, so they will enjoy that as well."

After some polite talk about a few other things, we drove to the area, which wasn't too large, but still appropriate for a modest zoo.

The Mayor introduced me to the future director of the zoo (who was his relative); and also to another of his cousins, who would work as the director of the restaurant.

I asked them what kind of animals they thought they could take care of, as some would require permanent supplies of meat, some would need vegetables, fruits, grains, etc., and he said, "No problem."

They even had a local vet who graduated from school in Saudi Arabia who would be the professional advisor.

So we planned a few enclosures. I had already checked with one of the largest zoos in Israel, and they were willing to donate some surplus equipment and animals to the Kalkilya Zoo.

In addition, a good friend of mine, Dr. Mordecai (Motke) Levison, a well-known, experienced Israeli vet, was also eager to cooperate.

After they finished building several enclosures with high fences, ditches, or moats, we gradually began to supply animals, along with very close supervision to be sure that the animals were being treated well.

The large variety of animals included a giraffe, zebra, lions, bears; a lot of parrots and even monkeys.

Because they didn't have money to build a modern zoo, we did as well as we could with a limited budget. And, although it resembled a zoo that might have been built in Europe in the 50s, with a lot of conventional-looking cages, what was important

127

was that the cages were appropriate for the animals and their safety (even though a hysterical ibex once succeeded—nobody knew how—to leap a wall that was 20 feet high).

One day, sometime later, I determined that two striped hyenas had to be removed from one of Israel's "animal schoolyards" because the conditions there were not good. I recommended that the Kalkilya zoo take them, although I didn't realize at the time that some Arab people have negative legends connected with hyenas.

For instance, they believed that hyenas get close to a village and would hypnotize someone to follow them for a few miles, and then turn on him and kill him.

So, after the two striped hyenas, which were very docile, were put in their new and quite nice enclosure, I came to visit them a couple of days later. To my shock, their whole enclosure was full of rocks and rubbish that visitors had thrown at them.

The zoo people told me, that, although the people were much attracted to the hyenas and were fascinated with them, the hatred of this animal was so big, it took them a few weeks to change their attitude and accept the hyenas as one of the local, very interesting animals.

Then, in the late 80s, when political demonstrations increased in the West Bank and there were many riots, we considered taking the animals back to Israel because we were afraid that, during the curfew, it would be difficult for anyone to give the zoo animals proper food and care.

But I was happily surprised that there was no problem.

In fact, a kind of coalition formed among all kinds of groups on the West Bank, to care for the animals, under difficulty; to work and bring food; and, even when the Israeli vet had to bring special medications to the zoo, he would change vehicles at the border so he would have a local license plate and wouldn't be a target.

In the late 80s, the Mayor was suspected by local groups of being a collaborator with Israel, so he had to change his name and disappear. He's been gone for a long time, maybe retired to a nearby country.

And, in spite of what is called "Intifada," to this day, the zoo that Israel helped build is a joy to the people of Kalkilya.

I think that this concept is an excellent bridge for peace: If you can learn to take care of animals, you might learn to take better care of people!

Afterwords

Reintroduction: To Be or Not To Be

More About the Author's Life
*My Early Life in Jerusalem
*My Life with Fish
*My Life at the Zoo
*My Life Today

Acknowledgments

Here's What They Said...

Recommended Reading

Reintroduction: To Be or Not To Be?

It may sound simple to go out and get some new animals to replace those that may have gone extinct from your country or from the world—but it's obviously a very complicated process.

First, we have to consider the question of why to reintroduce?

It may be a moral reason, i.e. in most cases, we were responsible for this animal's disappearance and it's only fair to get them back to their original place.

Second, the absence of an important component of the ecosystem causes it to be more fragile. Reintroduction contributes to the stabilization of the fragile system, and, from the scientific point of view, some of the animals are quite rare, and in order to preserve them we have to put them in a place where they can survive successfully.

Other major issues involve deciding which animals to add back to the country. What are the best locations from which to get them? Could it be a predator that would be dangerous to man and to his livestock? What is the potential of the animal becoming a pest? Will the animal affect the ecological balance? Where in the country would it fit? Can it be a carrier of new parasites that might affect other local animals? Can it disperse and have enough range to regenerate its population?

We also have to consider when it disappeared, and why?

So, in order to decide which animal and where, you have to know well the wild animals living in your own country and the ecology of the species you plan to reintroduce—as well as the reasons for their extinction.

Second, you have to consider the laws of the IUCN (The International Union for the Conservation of Nature and Natural Resources), the world's main authority on the conservation status of species, whose principle is, "the last to disappear should be the first to be reintroduced."

Third, you have to check where there is a similar ecological habitat from which to get these animals. Are these animals identical morphologically and physiologically? Who are their natural enemies? What kinds of food do they eat vs. what is available here? Is there an available water source? What kinds of parasites are present in the area from which we will get them?

And then you have to build a breeding nucleus of sufficient numbers of specimens from which the animals will be released back to the wild.

Different ways to release animals back to the wild

In many cases, we have to be careful that the process of release back to the wild is comparatively slow so the animals can get used to the local wild conditions where they will have to fend for themselves vs. the conditions at the breeding site where they were being well cared for.

After breeding, you may release one particular species as a group into the chosen habitat that has the proper ecological qualities; or you may release other species one-by-one, according to the typical behavior qualities of the animal, i.e. if the animals are loners, and can find their own way.

In the case of the Mesopotamian fallow deer, we built a special release enclosure for them at a dense natural Macquie (High Chaparral) forest in the Galilee near a natural water source and put them there for a year to let them get used to the natural plants, with nearly no human contact. They were protected from predators, but we didn't give them any hay or concentrated protein; we let them smell and feel the noises of the night with the jackals and other natural occurrences; we let them socialize and find their "place" within the herd; and, only after about a year, we opened the fence and let them go slowly back to nature, with special transmitters to let us follow them. We also attached mortality (motion) sensors to some of the animals to enable us to know if they were dead or alive.

"Hard release" is the method of releasing the animals one-by-one and letting them adapt as they go. This is what we did

134

with the roe deer. As roe deer are not social animals, we took them from the Hai-Bar breeding center and released them one-by-one without any acclimatization period and hoped that their native senses would protect them, lead them to the water sources, and help them survive.

Genetic variability of the animals

You must also take into consideration the genetic variability of the animals you bring back: If they are too identical genetically, mating between relatives might cause a higher percentage of defects, that is to say, higher medical and health problems.

In the case of reintroducing the Mesopotamian fallow deer to Israel, while they were NOT the last deer to disappear, they were considered "near extinct" globally, so we got them when we had the chance, which might have been missed forever if we had not acted then.

Years after many Mesopotamian fallow deer were released, we saw that they were in quite good physical condition, in spite of their close genetic composition, and they had spread all over, quite far from their original enclosure. Some of them even caused agricultural damage to the fruit plantations. But we estimated their numbers as increasing, and we saw a lot of young fawns that didn't have tracking collars, so we know they were born in the wild and the reproduction seemed successful.

Finally, in order not to put all the eggs in one basket, we also released a group of Mesopotamian fallow deer in a rich *wadi* (valley) in the center part of the country, not far from Jerusalem. We also put some specimens into some zoos to keep several sources if we needed them; and we still maintain breeding procedures at the Carmel Hai-Bar near Haifa.

We had hopes that, in the future, the Mesopotamian fallow deer might be a bridge for good relations with our neighbors, Jordan, Syria, and even Iraq, where these deer used to roam free, and had also completely disappeared.

135

Then there are times when you just can't get the identical species to the one that disappeared. So it took us quite a long time to decide about the reintroduction of the roe deer.

Although the roe deer was the last deer to go extinct from Israel, we couldn't get them from Iran, Syria, or Iraq for obvious reasons. The only available source for new stock was Europe, and the animals there were accustomed to entirely different ecological conditions than those in Israel.

Another reintroduction example is the onager. The typical onager that used to live in Israel, the Syrian onager, went extinct from the world at the beginning of the 20th century. And, as we had decided to add a large herbivore to the southern animal fauna of Israel, one which could serve as a food source (after his death) for birds of prey, we chose the Asiatic wild ass, a close relative to the local onager—as close as we could to the one that was extinct. At the beginning of the 80s, after a long and difficult process, we established a nice herd that is now roaming free in the southern arid area of Israel.

Later, we reintroduced the Arabian oryx, which we acquired from some leading American zoos, which are also now roaming free in the south.

Reintroductions don't always succeed

The first release of the ostrich failed. It wasn't a local species, but, like the onager, it was a close relative we got from the Danakil Desert in Ethiopia—but they all died. We're not sure exactly why, but we are trying to find the reasons. We may have to change either the way to introduce them, or the place to do it. We also did not succeed with the African wild ass, as their reproduction at the Hai-Bar south was not good.

What if a reintroduced animal is too successful?

Another dilemma was what to do with the wild goats we have at the Carmel Hai-Bar that were acquired from an Island near Crete some time in the 70s.

Wild goats once inhabited this country, domesticated by ancient man, but we don't know where. Remains have been found at historical sites, and we are not sure that this special goat is the one that used to be here, possibly the Persian wild goat. We also weren't exactly sure when the wild goat disappeared from our country.

On the other hand, wild goats can be a very important component of the ecosystem, as they eat a large variety of wild plants and they probably can survive without any water source.

Some zoologists are against wild goat reintroduction as they fear that they might be too successful and will cause irreversible damage to the vegetation. On the other hand, I think they would be preyed upon by the dense population of local jackals and the few wolves that we have, which would keep their numbers in balance. They can, however, also protect themselves from being preyed upon by climbing very steep rocky terrain where their predators can't reach them. So, until now, there is not a positive decision, and we keep them in an enclosure at the Carmel Hai-Bar.

Other creatures considered for reintroduction

We considered reintroduction of birds, but we had lost quite a few important species, such as the Lappet-faced vulture and the Ketupa, a nocturnal bird that eats fish. We weren't sure that the conditions that caused them to disappear had changed; and we couldn't find good sources from which to get them, especially from among countries that were hostile to our own existence, let alone worrying about the existence of animals.

And, although we didn't reintroduce any reptiles or amphibians, we built a nice pond (almost as nice as a Five-Star hotel) for fire salamanders in the Carmel Hai-Bar, as these interesting amphibians are the only salamander in this country, the southern edge of their global distribution limit.

Or, why might it be important to reintroduce a creature like the leech? Nowadays in our country, we can't find, except in a very few places, medicinal leeches, which used to be fairly common, probably because most water sources are not clean enough any more. This situation prevents us from bringing them back, as the cause for their disappearance is still present. Yet, we know that they are being used in a few projects or research. Scientists milk them and use the special chemical called "*hirudin*" that they produce to treat blood clots, thrombosis, or even some kind of cancers. We need to think about taking care of polluted water sources, knowing that even leeches need special conditions in order to survive.

No control over the reintroduction

Sometimes we have no control over reintroduction. For example, many fish species migrated from the Red Sea to the Mediterranean via the Suez Canal (The Lessepsian Migration). We couldn't do a thing to control it. They had to pass through the Bitter Lakes near the Suez Canal, some of which have very high salinity. Once they successfully passed through the Suez Canal, they might have met up with a competitive local species, or new and different salinities, or different temperatures and food. So, many of them did not make it, but a few managed to establish local stable populations which grew larger and larger and can now be found along most Mediterranean coasts. One of them is a small Red Sea barracuda; the other is a special red mullet. We were also surprised to discover the American blue crab, which came to our coast from the United States with the help of the fouling on the bottom of ships (called Sea Beard), and is now a regular citizen of our coast.

Another time I discovered a huge grouper, which, in the Red Sea gets to as much as 250 kilograms (more than 500 pounds).

Although we found a few specimens of this grouper along the Mediterranean coast, they disappeared after a year, likely because they couldn't adapt.

When it comes to reintroduction, I think about the similarities with the first Jews who came to Palestine from Eastern Europe in the early 20th Century: They had to tackle a local hostile population, different food, different temperature, and different parasites. And although many died during this process, the ones who survived also demonstrate the survival of the fittest.

Finally, I think we should emphasize better follow up on the mammals and birds that have been released. We need more, large, nature reserves; more restrictions on hunting; and funds to add more manpower with Jeeps, so we can follow up on the animals during and after the acclimatization period.

More About the Author's Life

My Early Life in Jerusalem

I'm a seventh generation "*sabra*" (native-born Israeli), the first baby born at Hadassah Hospital on Mount Scopus, in 1939, and I grew up in Jerusalem in the 1940s.

My mother's ancestors came from Austro-Hungary to Palestine in the 1700s. Her maiden name was Ahuva Goldberg, and her mother's maiden name was HaCohen. I understand that my mother's grandfather was a coffee grinder and a writer in Palestine in the 1800s.

My father, Isidore, who had studied in Danzig, Germany, was a building engineer who came to Palestine from Russia at the beginning of the 1930s. His family, the Lourie side of my name, is thought to be one of earliest Jewish families coming out of Padua, Italy, in the 12th century; later moving to Russia; and eventually to Palestine in the 1930s.

All my father's siblings (five boys and one girl) left Russia during or after the war between the Red and the White. They had taken the White side, and even lost one of their brothers in this war.

I grew up in one of the first neighborhoods built outside the wall of old Jerusalem. In our neighborhood, called Shchoonat Montefiore (near Beit Hakerem), there were about 30 to 40 families, a synagogue, and one kindergarten. We had neighbors about 50 meters away on one side of our house, and about 100 meters away on the other side.

Our House

I lived with my parents, my mother's father, Asher, and my mother's sister's family in a huge house my grandfather built at the beginning of the 1930s. One of my mother's brothers was an amateur architect and he helped with the plans. The walls, built from solid Jerusalem stone, were at least one foot thick. The house was huge and cool. We each had our own room. And we had running water.

My mother, Ahuva, knew German perfectly and attended a special seminary for teachers in Tel Aviv. She was known for her ability to work with poor and problem children. That must have been why the Chief Inspector of the Ministry of Education selected her when she was just 20 years old to teach in one of the poorest neighborhoods in Jerusalem—a demonstration school for other teachers to see how to run classes in similar settings.

Although both my parents—who married late in life—were very busy, I have happy memories of my father sitting and reading with me and translating Captain Marvel comics from English. It was good because the good people always won, not like in life where bad things happen to you.

Outside our house we had a very big garden with a large variety of vegetables—lettuce, eggplant, onions, tomatoes, parsley, radishes, and more. We had a few chickens, from which we would get eggs. We also had a lot of fruit trees with a taste of the past, including very good Arab plums, and the only cherry tree in Jerusalem. The yard included a few Arab Jasmine shrubs and a violet lilac bush, which was one of very few lilacs in Jerusalem. Newcomers from Eastern Europe would often come to our yard to savor the fine fragrance of the lilacs, and appreciated the gift of a bouquet of branches to take home.

Our large yard also boasted about forty tall pine trees—and under these pines were a lot of "pine mushrooms," which we ate. I found lots of wild and tasty, safe-for-eating mushrooms in the fields nearby.

My Grandfathers

My mother's father, Asher Goldberg, who lived with us, was one of my best friends. A goat shepherd in his early life, he was a widower with ten children who grew up in a cave-like home in old Jerusalem. My mother was very dedicated to him because her mother was dead and she felt she needed to look after him. After he had his own butcher shop, my grandfather earned enough money to build the house in which I grew up, outside the walls of Old Jerusalem.

I remember that my grandfather would go to the synagogue every Saturday, and that he was always holding a bible or prayer book, always reading and always praying, his lips moving silently.

When I was sick with *scarlatina* (scarlet fever), I had to stay in bed for six months. So when my parents went to work every morning, my dear grandfather was my babysitter. After he'd get tired of telling me stories about his early days as a shepherd, he'd make me oregano tea and suggest that we play a game of cards. We mainly played an Arab card game with a lot of calculations, so I learned a bit about mathematics from this. More important, perhaps, is that he didn't ever let me win; I think he even cheated me a little. Maybe that explains why, to this day, I don't like card games very much.

He had some other interesting habits: He liked cracking a whip and he used local leeches for his health, a practice that I have already mentioned in one of my stories.

When my grandfather was about 80 years old, doctors discovered that his heart was completely on the right side of his chest. The staff doctors of the leading hospital in Jerusalem wanted his permission to dissect him after his death and study it. I still remember that the doctors would come every few months and visit him, and he would wait with a bucket of water, like a child. As they approached, he would try and throw the water at them, because he knew what they were going to ask him, and he always refused.

My other grandfather on my father's side, David Lourie, had a huge mustache and also some unusual behaviors. He was way ahead of his time—a crazy vegetarian naturalist who ate almonds, was very good at preparing olives, and he liked taking long walks.

I understand that when he lived in Russia he was quite well off. He owned a wood factory where matches were made, and a bank. He was a White Russian and even a friend of the Tsar, but he lost all his wealth, everything, before he came to Palestine.

Nevertheless, my grandfather David was always writing letters to famous people like Stalin, Churchill, and Roosevelt, presumably to give them advice about how to run the world. And sometimes he even got replies!

I spent many days at my Russian grandfather's place, with him and my grandmother, Shifra. She'd make beet borscht, and he would tell me all sorts of things about a vegetarian way of life. Then he'd talk about the big place they had in Russia, and about his letters to the big shots, and he always gave me a *ruble* (a Russian coin) as a present.

My Aunt's Family

My mother's sister, Esther, lived with us, along with her husband and their only son. Once, when I was about seven years old, my uncle—who was a well-known psychologist and should have known better—took one of my favorite tortoises without telling or asking me, and gave it to his son. I immediately took it back; it was mine after all, and one of my favorites. But I was so shocked at what he did that I didn't speak to my uncle for a number of years.

The War of Independence—1948

After Israel was declared a legitimate state by the United Nations, the War of Independence began. I was about nine years old at that time. There were a lot of airplane and cannon attacks on our neighborhood by our Arab neighbors because there was an ammunition supply depot not far from our house, which they wanted to destroy. They kept bombing the whole area because they didn't know exactly where the depot was located.

Our cellar became a *meeklat* (a bomb shelter). It housed a large water reservoir (cistern), which collected the rain and also had a huge, covered hole for sewage, which was emptied once a year. We were lucky to have the water hole in the basement, and we gave water to most of our neighbors during the war.

During the attacks, our house was hit by more than ten shells, but only a few pieces of stone went missing, because the house was built so solidly. There were air raid sirens nearly every day and we couldn't go out for any length of time due to the frequent shelling.

On the other hand, on more than one occasion I was asked to "run" messages between some of the outposts in our area. Once, a shard of rock, shattered by a bullet, hit my back and tore my shirt; it was a very close call. A bomb dropped from an airplane killed the younger brother of a close friend of mine—this was my first "meeting" with death.

I'd go out mostly during the day—after school or on the weekends. I tried not to go too far so I would be able to run back quickly to our shelter. I couldn't contact close friends because they were too far away, so I would go to the fields. When there was shelling nearby, I would lie flat in the field, sometimes holding a "friendly" rock to keep me company.

This was the period when I first began to be a collector. I was not really aware of the danger when I decided I wanted to have the largest collection of different shell casings of different brands, as the Israeli army had a large variety of guns—Italian, English, Canadian, Czechoslovakian—with varying diameters.

I mentioned that my grandfather David would walk every day for miles. However, when he was walking during the war, in 1948, he got hit by a piece of shrapnel, and died a few weeks later.

The Beginning of My Lifelong Interest in Animals

As a curious, independent eight-year-old growing up in Jerusalem without many other children around—and without much supervision from my parents—I spent most of my time playing alone in the nearby fields, and created a nice collection of animals and insects and fossils (sea urchins, snails, ammonites) at my home.

In my room I had few toys, few books, and lots of jars full of spiders, crickets, lizards, scorpions; a very young tortoise (fresh out of the egg and getting special treatment); grasshoppers, and black beetles. In one big container was a beautiful caterpillar, the larva of a Swallowtail butterfly. I also kept a three-legged mouse I had found outdoors, nearly dead, that had gotten used to me.

Some of the containers didn't have proper covers, so many of the creatures easily found their way out. And once, one of them, a big spider, bit my mother's upper lip quite badly. I was so afraid and ashamed, I wanted to hide under the bed after this happened. She immediately took all the jars and threw them in the rubbish. (I of course immediately took them out of the rubbish and hid them until the atmosphere improved).

The fields near my home were very full of thorns and rocks and a few, very few, wild trees remained standing; most had been cut down by nearby villagers. I used to find scorpions and snakes and a lot of toad tadpoles there, which I was very happy to raise in big soup plates which I stole from my mother. I also noted and loved the many beautiful wildflowers which changed the dull color of the fields to a variety of bright reds, yellows, and purples.

And that was the beginning of my life with animals and nature.

My Life with Fish

Many think that people from Jerusalem—living so far from the sea—never learn how to swim. Then how did I end up being a Marine Biologist? Well, a typical getaway for a Jerusalem family is to go to the sea. When I went on vacation with my mother to the city of Nahariya, I taught myself to swim at a swimming pool there.

A number of years later, after I had a zoology degree from the Hebrew University in Jerusalem and two children and a wife to support, no one was looking to hire a zoologist. But I saw an ad in the paper that said: "Wanted: Zoologist needed for a new project about Mediterranean fish—no experience required."

I applied, met with the director of the Sea Fisheries Research Station in Haifa, and he agreed to hire me. So I moved my family to Haifa, rented an apartment, and began to get used to a new city, which I had hardly known until then, and which I now find to be an extremely nice place to live.

The first day I went to my new place of work, the fish laboratory at the Sea Fisheries Research Station, I met an elderly American woman zoologist, who, after checking my ability to dissect a large fish and identify some of the organs, said to me, "You will be an ichthyologist."

And that's how I began a new adventure in my life.

Migration of Fish

My job was to study fish that had migrated from the Red Sea into the Mediterranean via the Suez Canal. (This is called "The Lessepsian Migration" after Ferdinand de Lesseps, developer of the Suez Canal).

Several times a week, I would go to a harbor near Haifa, identify all the Mediterranean fish species, and also sail frequently on a research fishing vessel, learning how to use all kinds of fishing equipment and other scientific instruments for measuring water salinity, temperature, etc.

This project was financed by the American Navy to provide them with a lot of oceanographic data, not just about fish, but about submarines and other things that maybe I shouldn't mention.

I found that I was quite resistant to seasickness. Sometimes I had to sail for weeks to several places in the Mediterranean Sea to gather these measurements—I have to admit that I enjoyed it very much. Occasionally we went abroad to Rhodes, Cyprus, and other places for a couple of weeks.

The vessel was a conventional, but old and rusty fishing trawler, weighing about 70 tons and measuring about 20 meters long. It carried big piles of buoys and fishing nets and had a huge anchor.

This boat was also used for weeklong educational outings by students from Haifa studying marine subjects. Since they weren't accustomed to life on the water, they became seasick quite often and we could never get rid of that sour smell.

The crew consisted of people who knew how to operate the sophisticated scientific equipment: a captain, a cook, a mechanic and about six to eight researchers. Some specialized in fish, some in invertebrates and some were experts on the physical and chemical tools needed to measure temperatures, water salinity at different depths, and the like.

We had a very good cook on the ship, but one of the captains, who was Italian, was also quite interested in food.

From him I learned to eat a large variety of marine animals which he would prepare in very tasty Italian styles. Many of the sea creatures that the experimental nets brought up became our food.

For instance, we ate very unique squid and calamari and some fish that we knew from the Red Sea. Sometimes our nets would reveal other surprises—a cache of antique clay containers and old tools, and once even an old anchor from a sunken ship.

The navigation system on our ship was comparatively primitive, so one morning, on our way from the island of Rhodes to Haifa Harbor, we came quite close to Beirut,

Lebanon. It was a very foggy day, and we discovered our mistake when we saw the blinking tower light, which was different than the Haifa light. Although a few local Arab boats tried to approach us, we succeeded in escaping and got to Haifa safely. (After that incident, we bought more accurate and modern navigation equipment!)

Research Findings

For my research, I would use a special kind of fine net that could take samples of very small fish larvae, which were only a few days old. We also found unusual fish that were not known along our coast before, and they were full of bioluminescence. I would identify them later at the laboratory, with the help of old books and a lot of intuition.

I'd note their physical condition, length, etc., and collect all kinds of biological data. During my nine or ten years of doing this work, I identified nineteen species of deep-sea fish in the eastern Mediterranean Basin that had not been studied or noted previously.

Some others had originated from the Red Sea. For a fish to pass from the Red Sea to the Mediterranean is quite difficult. They had to pass the Bitter Lakes near the Suez Canal, some of which have very high salinity. Then they had to successfully pass through the Suez Canal and find their way to the Mediterranean coast, where they met, I believe, with competitive local species, as well as new and different salinities and temperatures.

Later, I specialized in deep-scattering layers of fish, and succeeded to get my Master's Degree based on studying young stages (larvae) of fish that had penetrated the Mediterranean and are now reproducing in our region.

A Temporary Distraction

Another memory I savor from when I was a marine biologist was of a beautiful Brazilian biologist who came for a short time to conduct a study at our laboratory. She was knock-out-drop-dead beautiful, but what attracted us most was a very unique fragrance that always accompanied her. We were in love with this smell, which was new to us, so on her last day, I dared to ask her, "What is the source of this smell that is driving us crazy?"

"Very simple," she answered... "It's a well-known French aftershave for men, called "Mustache."

Research on the Atlantis II and a New Friend

A few years later I was invited by the American Institute of Oceanography at Woods Hole to take part in a two-week research cruise in the Mediterranean, from Rhodes to Italy.

The ship was called Atlantis II, very large, and with a very large crew of more than a hundred. They were also searching for sea treasures with the help of some antique maps.

For me, it was like a floating hotel. I got to know and like typical American foods like hamburgers and hot dogs. The scientific equipment was very modern and sophisticated, and, with the help of a special TV camera, we could see the fish at the extreme depth of a few thousand meters, in certain layers.

Why they were there, and other data, were some of the questions which we tried to answer.

We found a large variety of fish, and also invertebrates (crustaceans, inkfish, calamari), which were quite unique; many of them had large teeth to catch food that was falling down from the layers above. The special patterns of bioluminescence on their skin, may have allowed them to identify their own kind as well as avoid their enemies.

On this boat, I made a new friend, Sneed Collard II, a marine biologist from the University of West Florida in Pensacola. A very nice man with a lot of humor and a lot of knowledge, he was quite interested in Israel, and, not only in the fish, but also our local fauna, like wolves and other kinds of mammals, which I knew quite well.

We spent a few days together in southern Italy where we enjoyed the typical tasty Italian food, went to some nightclubs, and nearly forgot about our families. Later, he visited my country, very interested in the work we did here, wanting to see some of the Mediterranean animals he had only read about. We went to military areas along the Egyptian coast of the Mediterranean captured by Israel after the Six-Day War and later released. Sneed even took part in guarding our small camp with an Uzi.

Sneed became a very good friend and stayed at my house when in Israel. We visited many nice places in the country together. Another time I visited him in Pensacola and got to know his family and children, who also later came to visit us in Israel.

I liked very much his humor; his open mind for different kinds of biological problems and phenomena; his deep contact with the students; and his ability to transfer to them his deep love for the marine animals.

We remained very good friends until his recent death, and I am now lucky to continue my friendship with his son, Sneed Collard III, who "got the proper genes" and became a major writer of children's books about biology.

My Life at the Zoo

How did I go from being a marine biologist doing research on fish of the Mediterranean to becoming the youngest zookeeper in the country at the Haifa Zoo?

Of course I always liked animals very much and I used to visit the zoo often as an interested Haifa citizen. At that time, the zoo consisted of a couple hundred animals, some of them very old, including rare Syrian bears, several kinds of monkeys (some without mates) and wolves held in a very small enclosure, without enough physical activity.

I fell in love with the zoo, not only because of the animals, but because it was located in a very beautiful natural area of Haifa overlooking the Mediterranean Sea—and finally, because it was modest and needed some help.

Working with Children

In 1969, on one of my visits to the zoo, I overheard the zoo director (Shlomo Farber) telling a group of students something about the mongoose that wasn't totally accurate, so I interrupted politely and suggested to him that "maybe it was a little different than he was saying."

He admitted that I was right and asked me to come to his office later because he wanted to show me something. When I went to his office, I found that he was very interested in hearing about my past experiences as a zoologist, my life when I was a boy, and my work as a marine biologist. I was amazed at his wide knowledge of physics and chemistry.

He told me there were a lot of young children who wanted to know more about animals, and that the zoo had a small budget from the Ministry of Education. He offered to give me a small salary if I would agree to meet with primary school children twice a week and teach them about nature. Even though I liked animals and children very much, I was curious about how I would be as a teacher, without any experience. But I thought this would be an excellent combination of my interests, so I said I'd try.

The zoo's program at that time was under the Ministry of Education and I succeeded, without too much trouble, to pass all the teaching examinations with quite high marks.

The work with the children was always in the afternoon, and I could do it after my regular daily work at the fish research station.

After a few meetings with some very nice children, grades four and five, I found that I really enjoyed teaching them. And they enjoyed learning about nature through a lot of games and activities we did together, such as collecting leaves, trying to guess which animals were under stones, and so on.

Invited to be Director

There was quite a large demand for these nature youth clubs at the time, so Shlomo asked me to add more days; after a year, he suggested that I become a permanent member of the zoo staff. I accepted, and in 1970 I was formally nominated by the chairman of the board of directors of the zoo—which was not yet connected to the Municipality of Haifa—to become the zoo director.

The sea fisheries research station where I had been working was going to be closed within a year anyway because there was no budget. They transferred the project to another organization, so I had to decide whether to continue as a fish biologist or to become a zoo director.

The decision was quite easy. And that's how I became one of the youngest directors of a zoo in Israel; a position I held until 1979.

Located in a *wadi* (a steep valley) winding down to the sea, the zoo was very clean, full of natural, wild vegetation, and wild animals of the area. It even had a natural cave which contained fruit bats. You could hear the howls of the jackals coming around every evening and occasionally you could meet a

153

Palestinian viper crossing a path or a salamander coming to the natural pond. The zoo also contained an educational center for biology teachers, a small nature museum, several large prehistoric dioramas and collections of the tools of the early Carmelitic man.

When I started as director, there was a lot of work to be done: The cages were very old; most of them badly rusted. Before I came to the zoo, a lot of people would throw stones at the animals just to arouse them. The previous director had been a good teacher, but his limited budget didn't give him much chance to enrich the zoo or change the cages into more modern enclosures. I tried to improve these things, but the process was slow because of high costs.

First, I established good relations with a local vet who helped me improve the veterinary treatment of the animals. I also connected with an experienced pathologist to learn what caused the death of some of the animals, so we could prevent unnecessary sickness and death.

I recognized the importance of working with children and nature, as well as the benefits of using animals to work with children. Some of the teachers that worked in the zoo's nature education center guided nature outings and helped children discover the reptiles, birds, insects and all kinds of invertebrates that were around. They helped show the children that there was a new world under the stones and taught them that no animals are really "bad." This nature education for children was new, very welcome, and very successful. I also tried to have regular, weekly programs to get the people living in Haifa to come for "nature lessons."

When the Municipality of Haifa eventually agreed to pay the salaries of some of the maintenance people, the place began to be called, "The Haifa Zoo."

My Life Today

I believe my constant contact with wild animals helped me to be more sensitive to others.

A lot of my time I practice on my nine grandchildren, trying to make them smile with the help of stories like those in this book.

I also go to needy children, elderly with limited physical or mental ability, and ex-convicts who are in the rehabilitation process and are distanced from normal society.

I try to show them all what might be missing in today's education—chances to see the beauty of, and develop more interest in, animals that are everywhere around us—spiders, snakes, the world in a puddle, the metamorphosis of a butterfly, or hundreds of other chances to observe how animals act and react to their world, and think about how we might learn from this.

Finally, I very much enjoy visiting flea markets, looking for old wristwatches, special old tools, and all kinds of things connected with Old Israel/Palestine.

Acknowledgements...

To everyone I've known, worked with, helped, or who helped me throughout my life: Mentors, co-workers, educators, family, friends, relatives, at-risk and differently-abled children and adults, homeless people and prisoners, to name a few. From each I've learned much. I've had so many wonderful, memorable, unusual, and, always rewarding, experiences. Here are a few to thank, with gratitude to many more...

I am so grateful for the privilege of working with the great Gen. Avraham Yoffe, first director of the Nature Reserves Authority; and then people like Salach, the Druze Shepherd, who nursed the Mesopotamian fallow deer from the original four to the largest herd in the world today...

The late Prof. Heinrich Mendelssohn, an influential figure in Israel's zoology, backed me in many important zoological dilemmas and decisions; we had many wonderful and interesting experiences together...

My wife and children were always VERY patient (and the children sometimes very happy), when, over the years, I brought home monkeys, bears, tigers, jackals, hyenas, snakes, scorpions, cockroaches, and so many others. Now my nine grandchildren keep me on my toes to tell them stories about everything...

My dear friend and publisher, Yoel Eizenberg said he would do anything to help me, and he did—much more than I can say...

Itamar Levy, well-known book expert consistently encouraged me to write this book...

Sneed Collard III, son of my late dear friend, Sneed Collard II, has been extremely generous with ideas and support...

Leah Broyde Abrahams of Mixed Media Memoirs LLC gave us tons of good advice, information, help, and guidance...

But, to tell the truth, nothing would have happened until Cissy became my "real boss" and encouraged me to sit down and tell her everything. She is the creative force behind this book, and, thanks to her, I can share my stories with you.

Here's what they said...

"His work is an important milestone for nature conservation in Israel."
Dr. Eliezer Frankenberg, Former Chief Scientist of Israel's Nature Reserves Authority, Jerusalem, Israel

"As someone who has accompanied Avi into the field as he educated new generations of Israelis about their native ecosystems, it's a joy to share the drama, humor, and insights packed into this riveting collection which other readers are sure to enjoy."
Sneed Collard III, Author and Publisher, Recipient of the Washington Post-Children's Book Guild Award for Nonfiction, Missoula, Montana

"Avinoam is leaving an amazing legacy with his work around the world."
Timothy Vargo, Manager of Research & Citizen Science, Urban Ecology Center, Milwaukee, Wisconsin

"He taught me that animals are just like people... treat them the same and treat them well."
A student's summary of Avinoam's message to eighth grade middle school class in Wildlife Conservation & Ecology, Green Bay, Wisconsin

"I always appreciated Avinoam's professionalism, his readiness to meet and greet guests that I would bring to the Hai-Bar Carmel, his ability to tell the story of the Nature Reserves Authority, and his descriptions of projects that needed support."
General Yitzhak Segev (Ret.), Ramat Gan, Israel

"Truly a special person... just like a brother... helps everyone— children, elderly, mentally and physically disadvantaged... brings love to everything he does."
Salach Makhladeh, Druze shepherd and "Godfather" of the Mesopotamian fallow deer, Haifa, Israel

"I've known Avinoam for more than forty-five years, and I still hesitate to enter his house because I never know what might greet me there."
Yoel Eizenberg, close personal friend, Haifa, Israel

"Many of our friends had dogs, cats, and other pets, but no one had a tiger, bear, or even a monkey! Although we lived in a small apartment in Haifa, we always had room for the animals, especially if it was a Syrian teddy bear, a monkey, or small tigers. After a while we got used to all kind of animals that might share our home, and for us it was quite normal. The tiger cub that came from the Circus had a good friendship with me; at the beginning of his time at the zoo when he got too big to keep at home, he would come to play with me; but after a while it became too risky to get inside his cage because I thought he might be hungry and forget our friendship from the past."
Dr. Barak Lourie (Avinoam's middle child), Haifa, Israel

"Our house was full of animals all the time—little tigers from the circus, a bunch of very dangerous snakes in front of the door to our house, a mongoose on our balcony, a marbled polecat in a suitcase, and so on. Sometimes we had to be very brave to hold these animals which were stinky, bit us, and not very friendly. Boring it was not! Today, my children love to hear Vovo's (Grandpa's) stories about animals and go to the fields with him to search for ants and snakes..."
Yael Lourie Gelberg (Avinoam's youngest child), Binyamina, Israel

Recommended...

For more information about the nature and animals of Israel, we recommend:

— Alon, Azaria (2003, 2008). *Israel National Parks and Nature Reserves.* Carta Jerusalem, Israel.

— Ferguson, W.W. (2002). *The Mammals of Israel,* Gefen Publishing House, Jerusalem, Israel.

— Israel Nature and Parks Authority and The Society for the Protection of Nature in Israel (2004). *The Red Book, Vertebrates in Israel.* Distributed by Gefen Publishing House, Jerusalem, Israel.

*****

To order copies of "*A Bear in My Bed & A Jackal in My Oven,*" and to set up interviews, lectures and book signings in the United States and Israel:

Naomi K. (Cissy) Shapiro
Creative Brilliance
Box 44237
Madison, WI USA 53744-4237
Phone: ~~608-821-6198~~
e-mail: cre8vNaomi@gmail.com